Finding Information in Science, Technology and Medicine

By
Jill Lambert
&
Peter A. Lambert

Europa Publications
Taylor & Francis Group plc

© Jill Lambert and Peter A. Lambert 2003
Published by Europa Publications Limited 2003
11, New Fetter Lane
London EC4P 4EE
United Kingdom
(A member of the Taylor & Francis Group)

Reprinted 2004

ISBN 0851424627

Contents

Acknowledgements

Legends

Illustration acknowledgements

1   How information is communicated 1

2   Searching the Web 15

3   Using libraries 30

4   Using bibliographic databases 44

5   Obtaining and organising information 87

6   Keeping up to date 102

7   The future 115

Index 120

About the authors

Jill Lambert BSc MA MCLIP is a Team Leader for Science & Engineering and Head of Public Services in the Library & Information Services (LIS) at Aston University.

Peter A. Lambert BSc PhD DSc is a Reader in Microbiology in the School of Life & Health Sciences at Aston University.

Acknowledgements

We would like to thank Andrew Cameron of the Library & Information Services and Graham Smith of the School for Life & Health Sciences at Aston University for their assistance with the figures. Our thanks are also due to all the organisations who generously allowed us to reproduce examples from their Web sites and publications.

Jill and Peter Lambert
August 2001

Dedication

For Catherine and Ian

Legends

Figure 1   *Article from an Institute of Physics journal*

Figure 2   *UK patent application*

Figure 3   *Communication of scientific, technical and medical information*

Figure 4   Google *advanced Web search. (The Google brand features are trademarks of Google, Inc.)*

Figure 5   Scirus *advanced search (product of Elsevier Science)*

Figure 6   BUBL LINK *selected internet resources*

Figure 7   BUBL LINK *nanotechnology*

Figure 8 and   EEVL – The Internet Guide to Engineering, Mathematics Computing

Figure 9   *Library Web page*

Figure 10   Kempe's Engineers Year-book

Figure 11   *Library catalogue record*

Figure 12   *Keyword search*

Figure 13   COPAC *home page*

Figure 14   COPAC *search results*

Figure 15   Index to Theses *simple search.*
(Reproduced with permission from: Index to theses www.theses.com,©Expert Information.)

Figure 16   *Abstract of a thesis.*
(Reproduced with permission from: Index to theses www.theses.com,©Expert Information.)

Figure 17   MEDLINE *record.*
(PubMed is a registered trademark of the US National Library of Medicine.)

Figure 18   INSPEC *record. (Used with the permission of the Institution of Electrical Engineers, EDINA and OVID Technologies Inc.)*

Figure 19   Medical Subject Headings (MeSH) *browser.*
(PubMed is a registered trademark of the US National Library of Medicine.)

Figure 20   Chemical Abstracts *index guide. (CAS information is reprinted by permission of the American Chemical Society.)*

Figure 21   *Examples of Boolean logic*

Figure 22   OCLC FirstSearch *browse index. (Reproduced with the permission of OCLC Online Computer Library Center, Inc.)*

Figure 23   *Journals index display. (Used with the permission of the Institution of Electrical Engineers, EDINA and OVID Technologies Inc.)*

Figure 24a   *Screen display from PubMed. (PubMed is a registered trademark of the US National Library of Medicine.)*

Figure 24b   *Screen display from PubMed. (PubMed is a registered trademark of the US National Library of Medicine.)*

Figure 24c   *Screen display from PubMed. (PubMed is a registered trademark of the US National Library of Medicine.)*

Figure 24d   *Screen display from PubMed. (PubMed is a registered trademark of the US National Library of Medicine.)*

Figure 25a   INSPEC *on* EDINA *using* OVID *search software. (Used with the permission of the Institution of Electrical Engineers, EDINA and OVID Technologies Inc.)*

Figure 25b   INSPEC *on* EDINA *using* OVID *search software. (Used with the permission of the Institution of Electrical Engineers, EDINA and OVID Technologies Inc.)*

Figure 25c   INSPEC *on* EDINA *using* OVID *search software. (Used with the permission of the Institution of Electrical Engineers, EDINA and OVID Technologies Inc.)*

Figure 25d   INSPEC *on* EDINA *using* OVID *search software. (Used with the permission of the Institution of Electrical Engineers, EDINA and OVID Technologies Inc.)*

Figure 25e   INSPEC *on* EDINA *using* OVID *search software. (Used with the permission of the Institution of Electrical Engineers, EDINA and OVID Technologies Inc.)*

Figure 25f   INSPEC *on* EDINA *using* OVID *search software. (Used with the permission of the Institution of Electrical Engineers, EDINA and OVID Technologies Inc.)*

Figure 25g   INSPEC *on* EDINA *using OVID search software.*
(Used with the permission of the Institution of Electrical
Engineers, EDINA and OVID Technologies Inc.)

Figure 25h   INSPEC *on* EDINA *using OVID search software.*
(Used with the permission of the Institution of Electrical
Engineers, EDINA and OVID Technologies Inc.)

Figure 25i   INSPEC *on* EDINA *using OVID search software.*
(Used with the permission of the Institution of Electrical
Engineers, EDINA and OVID Technologies Inc.)

Figure 26a   Science Citation Index (Web of Science) *on* MIMAS

Figure 26b   Science Citation Index (Web of Science) *on* MIMAS

Figure 26c   Science Citation Index (Web of Science) *on* MIMAS

Figure 26d   Science Citation Index (Web of Science) *on* MIMAS

Figure 26e   Science Citation Index (Web of Science) *on* MIMAS

Figure 26f   Science Citation Index (Web of Science) *on* MIMAS

Figure 27   ingenta Journals. *(Used with the permission of ingenta plc.)*

Figure 28   NISS *Library OPACS in HE*

Figure 29   *Interlibrary loan request card*

Figure 30   *Prentice-Hall electronic mailing list*

Figure 31   NISS *bookshops and publishers*

Figure 32   zetoc Alert

Figure 33   *OVID save current search screen.*
(Used with the permission of the Institution of Electrical
Engineers, EDINA and OVID Technologies Inc.)

Figure 34   COS Expertise *search screen*

Figure 35   COS Expertise *results screen*

Figure 36   *Agora demonstrator project*

Illustration acknowledgements

Figure 1   Reproduced from Smart Materials and Structures, 2000, with
                the permission of IOP (Institute of Physics) Publishing Limited
                and the author, Professor D. D. L. Chung.

Figure 2   Reproduced from UK Patent Application GB 2183592 A, 1985,
                with the permission of the Patent Office.

Figure 4   Reproduced from the Google Web site, with the permission of
                Google Inc. (Google brand features are trademarks of Google,
                Inc.)

Figure 5   Reproduced from the Scirus Web site, with the permission of
                Elsevier Science.

Figure 6   Reproduced from the BUBL Web site, with the permission of
                BUBL Information Services.

Figure 7   Reproduced from the BUBL Web site, with the permission of
                BUBL Information Services.

Figure 8   Reproduced from the EEVL Web site, with the permission of
                EEVL: the Internet Guide for Engineering, Mathematics
                and Computing.

Figure 9   Reproduced from the Library & Information Services (LIS)
                Web site, with the permission of the Library & Information
                Services, Aston University

Figure 10   Reproduced from Kempe's Engineers Year-book, section
                L12, Solar Energy by Professor T Muneer, with the
                permission of United Business Media International Limited.

Figure 11   Reproduced from Aston University's Web catalogue, with
                the permission of the Library & Information Services, Aston
                University and DS Ltd.

Figure 12   Reproduced from Aston University's Web Catalogue, with
                the permission of the Library & Information Services, Aston
                University and DS Ltd.

Figure 13   Reproduced from the COPAC Web site, with the permission
                of COPAC, CURL and JISC.

Figure 14   Reproduced from the COPAC Web site, with the permission
                of COPAC, CURL and JISC.

Figure 15   Reproduced from the Index to Theses Web site, with
                 permission from Index to Theses, Expert Information.

Figure 16   Reproduced from the Index to Theses Web site, with
                 permission from Index to Theses, Expert Information.

Figure 17   Reproduced from the PubMed Web site, with the permission
                 of the US National Library of Medicine.

Figure 18   Reproduced from the OVID version of the INSPEC database
                 on EDINA, with the permission of the Institution of
                 Electrical Engineers (IEE), Ovid Technologies, and EDINA.

Figure 19   Reproduced from the PubMed Web site, with the permission
                 of the US National Library of Medicine.

Figure 20   Reproduced from the CA Index Guide with the permission of
                 Chemical Abstracts Service, a division of the American
                 Chemical Society.

Figure 22   Reproduced from OCLC FirstSearch Web site, with the
                 permission of OCLC Online Computer Library Center, Inc.

Figure 23   Reproduced from the OVID version of the INSPEC database
                 on EDINA, with the permission of the Institution of
                 Electrical Engineers (IEE), Ovid Technologies and EDINA.

Figure 24 a–d   Reproduced from PubMed Web site, with the permission of
                 the US National Library of Medicine.

Figure 25 a–i   Reproduced from the OVID version of the INSPEC database
                 on EDINA, with the permission of the Institution of
                 Electrical Engineers (IEE), Ovid Technologies, and EDINA.

Figure 26 a–f   Reproduced from the Web of Science Web site, with the
                 permission of ISI and MIMAS.

Figure 27   Reproduced from the ingenta Journals Web site, with the
                 permission of ingenta plc.

Figure 28   Reproduced from the NISS Web site, with the permission of
                 NISS, (NISS is a division of EduServ).

Figure 29   Reproduced with the permission of Library & Information
                 Services, Aston University.

Figure 30   Reproduced from the Prentice Hall Web site, with the
                 permission of Prentice Hall, a Pearson Educational Company.

Figure 31   Reproduced from the NISS web site, with the permission of
                 NISS (NISS is a division of EduServ).

Figure 32   *Reproduced from the zetoc Web site, with the permission on MIMAS*

Figure 33   *Reproduced from the OVID version of the INSPEC database on EDINA, with the permission of the Institution of Electrical Engineers (IEE), Ovid Technologies Inc. and EDINA.*

Figure 34   *Reproduced from the COS Web site, with the permission of Community of Science.*

Figure 35   *Reproduced from the COS Web site, with the permission of Community of Science.*

Figure 36   *Reproduced from the Agora demonstrator Web site, with the permission of the Agora Project and Fretwell Downing.*

Chapter 1

How information is communicated

Our purpose in writing this book is to help students and researchers in scientific, technical and medical fields to find information. Before we begin to outline the methods and techniques used to find information, we must first take one step back and consider how information in these subject fields is communicated. This information, generated by a variety of organisations including industrial and commercial enterprises and academic and government institutions, reaches the outside world through several different channels. Searching for information is easier once you know what these channels are and how they interlock to form a communication system.

People

The first obvious but very important way of spreading information is by word of mouth and email. People talk and email their friends and colleagues, passing on news about their own work and often including pieces of information they have read elsewhere. Information is also spread in this way in a more organised fashion by discussions at seminars, conferences and so on.

Picking up information from colleagues and going to meetings is very popular. The reasons are simple enough – it is far more convenient to ask someone working in the same field for facts than it is to search through a mass of information, and easier to learn about new work at a meeting than to read about it either in print or on screen. The snag with transferring information in this way is that it can only reach a very limited number of people. If you need to know something and your contacts cannot help, you have a problem. That is why other electronic and printed methods of communicating information, which can reach a large audience, are also needed.

The Web, email, discussion lists and usenet newsgroups

As you would expect, the Internet is widely used as a communication channel. Many research groups have set up Web sites summarising their areas of study, the facilities and equipment available to them, and giving some indication as to where they receive funding from, such as government agencies. The sites usually give the names of the main people in the research group, and a list of the papers they have published, along with their email addresses. In addition to acting as a "showcase" for their work, the sites are seen as being useful in helping to recruit postgraduate students, and more funding for new research projects. Web sites of professional institutions, learned societies, government departments, international organisations and companies now also play a large role in the communication of information in scientific, technical and medical subject fields.

In the public sector, collaborative projects with researchers located in different institutions, sometimes in different countries, are commonplace. Email is widely used by such researchers, for example to exchange experimental data or discuss the results of a clinical trial. Such communication would be private because of the need to maintain confidentiality before the results of a research project are published formally in journals.

There is also some use of discussion – or mailing – lists. These enable a group of people with a shared interest to communicate by joining an email discussion group. If you join a discussion list you receive every message sent to that list's address. Likewise any message you send will be received by everyone else on the list. The type of use made of discussion lists includes:

- establishing contact with other researchers active in the same subject field, especially for a newcomer, or for someone working in an isolated environment
- keeping up to date with news of all kinds – the latest developments in a subject, forthcoming meetings and conferences, or vacancies for research posts and jobs
- finding out if information on a topic is already available, the 'Can anyone help with...?' type of enquiry.

Usenet newsgroups have been likened to Internet public notice boards. Any messages sent can be read by anyone interested in the newsgroup. People reading the message can either respond to the sender privately by email, or publicly by "posting" their reply to a newsgroup. Although there are a very large number of groups, a hierarchical naming system is used for the first part of the name, to indicate the broad subject content. For example, *bionet.* is used for biological topics, and *comp.* for computing discussions.

Journals

New research which does not have to be kept secret for commercial or defence reasons is usually published in the form of articles or papers in journals. There are a large number of journals publishing research in this way, and they range in scope from very general ones covering the whole field of science to the very specific, covering small subject specialisms. Some are published by learned societies and professional institutions such as the Royal Society of Chemistry and the Institution of Mechanical Engineers, while others are the product of commercial publishers such as Blackwell, Elsevier, Wiley-Interscience and Academic Press.

Before an article is considered worthy of publishing it has to be refereed, that is evaluated or peer-reviewed by expert workers in the subject field. Refereeing practices vary between journals. Generally articles are evaluated by two independent assessors, who are looking for originality, validity and quality.

Most of the space in these journals is taken up by full articles having a well-defined format, with an introduction in which previous work is outlined and the objective of the research project indicated. The introduction is followed by a section outlining the experimental work conducted and any special methods used, the results, and the conclusions, discussing their significance and value. Where the findings are more limited, these are sometimes published as short articles, usually four to five pages in length. Figure 1 shows part of the first page of an article in the journal *Smart Materials and Structures*, published by the Institute of Physics.

The refereeing procedures plus the time required for editing, printing and binding mean that most articles are published between three and nine months after their submission. Where authors want research made public very quickly, perhaps because they believe it to be particularly significant or because there are rival teams working in the same field, they can attempt to publish the work in the form of a preliminary communication or letter. Such communications tend to have fairly brief introductory and experimental sections, concentrating on the results and conclusions which can be drawn from the work. In order to reduce publication delays, refereeing procedures are usually accelerated for such communications. It is assumed, however, that

Smart Mater. Struct. 9 (2000) 389–401. Printed in the UK

PII: S0964-1726(00)12007-5

Cement-matrix composites for smart structures

D D L Chung

Composite Materials Research Laboratory, State University of New York at Buffalo, Buffalo.
NY 14260-4400, USA

Received 22 November 1999, in final form 21 January 2000

Abstract. Cement-matrix composites for smart structures are reviewed. The functions include strain sensing, damage sensing, temperature sensing, thermoelectricity, vibration reduction and radio wave reflection. The functions are rendered by the use of admixtures, such as short carbon fibers, short steel fibers and silica fume.

1. Introduction

Smart structures are important due to their relevance to hazard mitigation, structural vibration control, structural health monitoring, transportation engineering and thermal control. Research on smart structures has emphasized the incorporation of various devices in a structure for providing sensing, energy dissipation, actuation, control or other functions. Research on smart composites has emphasized the incorporation of a smart material in a matrix material for enhancing the smart function or the durability. Research on smart materials has emphasized the study of materials (e.g. piezoelectric materials) used for making the devices. However, relatively little attention has been given to the development of structural materials (e.g. concrete) that are inherently able to provide some of the smart functions, so that the need for embedded or attached devices is reduced or eliminated, thereby lowering cost, enhancing durability, increasing the functional volume and minimizing mechanical property degradation (which usually occurs in the case of embedded devices).

Smart structures are structures that have the ability to sense certain stimuli and be able to respond to the stimuli in an appropriate fashion. Sensing is the most fundamental aspect of a smart structure. A structural composite which is itself a sensor is multifunctional.

This article reviews cement-matrix structural composites for smart structures. The smart functions addressed include strain sensing (for structural vibration control and traffic monitoring), damage sensing (both mechanical and thermal damage in relation to structural health monitoring), temperature sensing (for thermal control, hazard mitigation and structural performance control), thermoelectricity (for thermal control and energy saving), vibration reduction (for structural vibration control) and electromagnetic radiation reflection (for lateral guidance in highways).

Cement-matrix composites include concrete (containing coarse and fine aggregates), mortar (containing fine aggregate, but no coarse aggregate) and cement paste (containing no aggregate, whether coarse or fine).

Other fillers, called admixtures, can be added to the mix to improve the properties of the composite. Admixtures are discontinuous, so that they can be included in the mix. They can be particles, such as silica fume (a fine particulate) and latex (a polymer in the form of a dispersion). They can be short fibers, such as polymer, steel, glass or carbon fibers. They can be liquids such as methylcellulose aqueous solution, water-reducing agent, defoamer, etc. Admixtures for rendering the composite smart while maintaining or even improving the structural properties are the focus of this article.

2. Background on cement-matrix composites

Cement-matrix composites for smart structures include those containing short carbon fibers (for sensing strain, damage and temperature, for thermal control and for electromagnetic radiation reflection), short steel fibers (for sensing temperature and for thermal control) and silica fume (for vibration reduction). This section provides background on cement-matrix composites, with emphasis on carbon fiber cement-matrix composites due to its dominance among inherently smart cement-matrix composites.

Carbon-fiber cement-matrix composites are structural materials that are quite rapidly gaining in importance due to the decrease in carbon-fiber cost [1] and the increasing demand of superior structural and functional properties. These composites contain short carbon fibers, typically 5 mm in length, as the short fibers can be used as an admixture in concrete (whereas continuous fibers cannot be simply added to the concrete mix) and short fibers are less expensive than continuous fibers. However, due to the weak bond between the carbon fiber and the cement matrix, continuous fibers [2–4] are much more effective than short fibers in reinforcing concrete. Surface treatment of carbon fiber (e.g. by heating [5] or by using ozone [6, 7], silane [8], SiO$_2$ particles [9] or hot NaOH solution [10]) is useful for improving the bond between the fiber and the matrix, thereby improving the properties of the composite. In the case of surface treatment by ozone or silane, the improved bond is due to

389

Figure 1: Article from an Institute of Physics journal

these will be followed later by full articles, although in practice this is by no means always the case. The term "letters" in a journal title indicates that the articles are of a preliminary nature. Many journals publish a mixture of all three types of articles – full, short and preliminary. Some, for example *Biochemical and Biophysical Research Communications*, consist solely of preliminary communications.

Not all journals limit themselves to publishing research articles in the form outlined. Some journals concentrate on picking out the more interesting new developments and presenting these in a readable manner. Two of the most familiar are *New Scientist* and *Scientific American*, but there are many more specialised ones, particularly within engineering. Apart from the fact that they make interesting reading, these journals can be useful because new products are widely advertised in them.

Although print is still the main form of production, more and more publishers are now making electronic versions of their journals available via the World Wide Web (WWW). This can speed up the publishing process, with papers being able to be viewed well before the print version appears. With the journal *Smart Materials and Structures*, for instance, articles are made available in the online version as soon as they are ready for publication, which can be weeks or months before the print version is complete. Another way of speeding up publication is the "Papers in Press" approach. The *Journal of Biological Chemistry* – a prestigious title with a large readership – is making articles available electronically as soon as these have been peer-reviewed, before being copy-edited by the publisher's staff.

Electronic archives

The use of journals as a means of announcing new research started over 300 years ago. Over the last 20 years or so, however, the cost of scientific, technical and medical journals has risen dramatically. While higher prices have inevitably resulted in a downturn in the number of journals taken by libraries, they have also had the effect of encouraging the setting-up of electronic or "e-print" archives.

An e-print archive – other names include a "pre-print server" or "network" – is an electronic collection of research papers, accessible free on the Internet. In itself this is not essentially any different from the electronic versions of journals, mentioned in the previous section. However, all the papers in an electronic version of a journal will have been through the peer-review system before being published on the Web. With an e-print archive there is no guarantee that the paper has been refereed – some papers may have already been published in a journal, some accepted and awaiting publication, some posted to receive comments from other researchers before being submitted to a journal, and some never formally published at all.

The largest and best known is the *"arXiv"* e-print archive, based at Los Alamos National Laboratory in New Mexico. Set up in 1991, this archive now contains over 155,000 articles in physics, mathematics, computer science and non-linear systems (*http://www.arxiv.org*). More e-print archives are gradually being established in other subject fields in science, medicine and engineering, though not all will operate in exactly the same way. For instance *PubMed Central*, a repository sponsored by the US National Institutes of Health (*http://www.pubmedcentral.nih.gov/index.html*) has been established with two aims – to cover peer-reviewed papers already published in journals and non-refereed reports. Some of these non-refereed reports are genuinely pre-prints, in the process of being refereed for publication in conventional journals. Others though are reports, which will never go through the peer-review process, but are included because they are considered to provide valuable information for researchers.

One important benefit of an e-print system is the speed with which researchers can make their work public knowledge – there need be no time lag before publication. Another advantage is that authors can update their work at any point in the future. However, whether e-print collections can establish themselves fully as part of mainstream publishing will partly depend on the reputation they can establish, and partly on attracting enough papers. A high reputation is vital – the most important factor for a researcher in considering where to submit a paper for publication is the perceived value of a journal within the scientific, technical and medical community. Another factor which may deter researchers is the attitude adopted by journal editors. Some editors will not include papers in their journals if the results have already been posted on an e-print server, because they view this as "prior publication".

Theses

Much of the research published in journals is carried out by students working for higher degrees. This work has to be written up in the form of a thesis or dissertation, so that it can be assessed by external examiners. Theses can be good sources of information because the first chapter is always a state-of-the-art review of the subject, backed up by a comprehensive list of references to previous work.

Conference proceedings

Very often the research reported at conferences is later published as proceedings, sometimes in the form of a book, sometimes as separate papers in a journal. Conference proceedings can be a useful way of finding out about projects still in progress, which have not been written up in complete form as papers in journals. Conferences tend to focus on expanding subject fields or themes which are becoming increasingly important, so the published proceedings often reflect the future direction of a speciality. One note of caution though: published proceedings – at least those published in book form – are not usually refereed as are papers published in journals. The data may not therefore have been subjected to the same critical scrutiny.

Reports

A significant proportion of applied research and development is first written up in the form of reports. Some reports are made openly available to anyone interested but, where the work is of commercial or military value, they are restricted to a strictly specified limited number of people.

When reading reports it is worth remembering, as with conference proceedings, that the information has not been externally refereed or peer-reviewed. Much of the information which first appears in reports is in fact later published in journals, but in condensed versions. If you have a paper in which reference is made to an earlier report on the topic, it could be worth getting hold of this because of the extra detail included.

Patents

Industrial – and increasingly academic – research and development which has commercial value is normally published as patents. These are documents granted by governments to the owners of an invention, allowing them a monopoly for a limited period of time in order to exploit the invention. In return for this monopoly, the owners have to disclose (that is, make public) all the information available about the invention. Obtaining a patent is quite a lengthy and complicated affair since the invention has to be examined by a government's patent office. In the UK the first information is generally published about 18 months after submission as a patent application (Figure 2). The patent application is then formally examined and, if accepted, is republished as a complete specification later.

To be patentable, an invention must be:

- new – no information should ever previously have been published about the invention before the application has been filed
- require an inventive step – meaning that the invention should not already be obvious to someone with knowledge and experience of the area
- able to be made or used – for example, a new substance, material, device or apparatus.

Work that is not patentable includes:

(12) **UK Patent Application** (19) **GB** (11) **2 183 592** (13) **A**

(43) Application published 10 Jun 1987

(21) Application No 8529441

(22) Date of filing 29 Nov 1985

(71) Applicant
Arthur Guinness Son & Company (Dublin) Limited,

(Incorporated in Irish Republic),

St. James's Gate, Dublin 8, Republic of Ireland

(72) Inventors
Alan James Forage,
William John Byrne

(74) Agent and/or Address for Service
Urquhart-Dykes & Lord, 47 Marylebone Lane,
London W1M 6DL

(51) INT CL⁴
B65D 25/00 5/40

(52) Domestic classification (Edition I)
B8D 12 13 19 7C 7G 7M 7P1 7PY SC1
B8P AX
U1S 1106 1110 1111 B8D B8P

(56) Documents cited
GB 1266351

(58) Field of search
B8D
B8P
Selected US specifications from IPC sub-class B65D

(54) Carbonated beverage container

(57) A container for a beverage having gas (preferably at least one of carbon dioxide and inert (nitrogen) gases) in solution consists of a non-resealable container 1 within which is located a hollow secondary chamber 4, eg a polypropylene envelope, having a restricted aperture 7 in a side wall. The container is charged with the beverage 8 and sealed. Beverage from the main chamber of the container enters the chamber 4 (shown at 8a) by way of the aperture 7 to provide headspaces 1a in the container and 4a in the pod 4. Gas within the headspaces 1a and 4a is at greater than atmospheric pressure. Preferably the beverage is drawn into the chamber 4 by subjecting the package to a heating and cooling cycle. Upon opening the container 1, eg by draw ring/region 13, the headspace 1a is vented to atmosphere and the pressure differential resulting from the pressure in the chamber headspace 4a causes gas/beverage to be ejected from the chamber 4 (by way of the aperture 7) into the beverage 8. Said ejection causes gas to be evolved from solution in the beverage in the main container chamber to form a head of froth on the beverage. The chamber 4 is preferably formed by blow moulding and located below beverage level by weighting it or as a press fit within the container 1 by lugs 6 engaging the container walls, the container being preferably a can, carton or bottle. The chamber 4 may initially be filled with gas, eg nitrogen, at or slightly above atmospheric pressure, the orifice being formed by laser boring, drilling or punching immediately prior to locating the chamber 4 in the container 1.

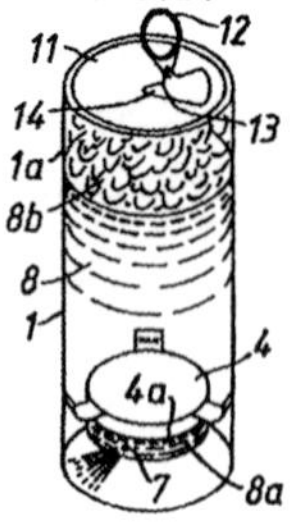

The drawings originally filed were informal and the print here reproduced is taken from a later filed formal copy.

FIG.5.

GB 2 183 592 A

Figure 2: UK patent application

- scientific theories
- mathematical methods
- computer programs
- methods of diagnosis
- methods of treatment by surgery
- a new animal or plant variety.

Despite the large numbers of patents in existence, it must be acknowledged that, until recently at least, patents have not been a popular information source for researchers. Problems are experienced with the legal style, and there are complaints about inadequate descriptions and implausible claims. There does seem to be a general belief that the work will later appear as papers in journals or conference proceedings. This does not appear to be the case in practice – it has been estimated that about 85% of the information in patents is never published elsewhere. Although it may not be easy to extract the information contained in patents, to ignore their existence is unwise.

Trade literature

Trade literature – advertisements, catalogues and company magazines – is a well-used source of information, particularly in engineering and construction. It contains the kind of practical information not published in more conventional literature, and also has the plus point of (normally) being well presented and illustrated.

Standards

Most of the methods of communication outlined so far are used to spread information about new research and development. Standards are different: they do not communicate new facts but specify acceptable dimensions in a product, set acceptable levels of quality or codify good existing practices. The most familiar, at least in the UK, are those produced by the British Standards Institution, but there are many other organisations, worldwide, which are also involved in formulating standards.

Books

The most familiar of all the printed methods of spreading information is, of course, books. Books do not report directly on new research or development: their publication schedule would be too slow and the information content of the average research paper would be too specialised to be of interest to sufficient readers to make a book economically viable. What the author of a book does is to repackage and evaluate information which has already appeared in a lot of different publications, which makes the book very useful when you need an introduction to an unfamiliar topic or to check a fact.

Reviews

Another way of drawing together information appearing in journals, conference proceedings and so on is by means of a review: a critical evaluation of the developments which have taken place in a speciality. Reviews are very highly regarded as information sources by researchers because they are written by acknowledged experts, and are well provided with references to further readings.

Reviews can be found singly in all sorts of publications – journals, conference proceedings and so on – and also collected together in separate review serials. These usually have easily recognisable titles such as *Annual review in...*, *Advances in...*, *Trends in...* and *Progress in....*

Bibliographic databases

All these different channels of communication are potential sources of information. The problem is how to find what you want among the mass of irrelevant items. One method of finding information on a topic would be to look at as many relevant journals as possible. Another method might be to browse through any conference proceedings available. Searching in this way is not very systematic – it can take a long time and the result will depend very much on what material is actually on the shelves or accessible electronically via your library or information centre.

A much more efficient, effective way of searching is to use bibliographic databases. These databases – often colloquially referred to as abstracts or indexes – summarise papers appearing in many different journals. Many also include conference proceedings, and some include reports and patents. Many bibliographic databases are produced for the scientific, technical and medical fields – virtually every subject is now covered by one or more. The databases are usually updated frequently, either weekly, fortnightly or monthly, an important point in terms of keeping up to date with new research. As Figure 3 shows, databases play a major role in the network by which scientific, technical and medical information is communicated.

Factual databases

All the sources of information outlined so far are mainly textual in content. Articles in journals, for instance, include data from experiments, but presented as part of a narrative script. Factual databases or databanks – the terms are used interchangeably – in contrast, can basically be described as numerical, such as the melting points of compounds, or

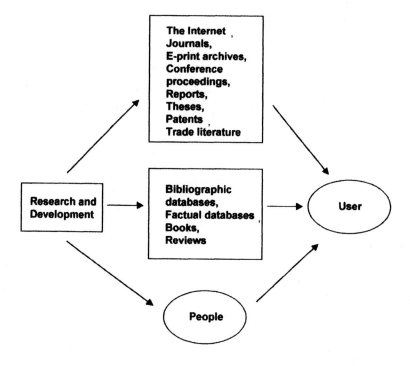

Figure 3: Communication of scientific, technical and medical information

chemical structures. Perhaps the most well known is the Human Genome Project (HGP) *(http://www.genome.gov/)*. The primary aim of the project is to build up the detail of the structure, location and function of the 30,000 or so genes in the human body. In fact the HGP is not simply one enormous databank, but a large number of separate, interlinked ones covering gene structure, sequence, maps and other related aspects.

Referencing

Before outlining the practical methods you can use to find information, it is worth briefly mentioning how work is cited, that is, referred to or acknowledged in publications. There are two different ways of citing references:

- The numeric system, in which each publication referred to is given a separate number; for example, "Further work [9] has shown" or "Further work by Jones [9] has shown". The numbers can also be given as superscripts. The references are then listed in full in numerical order at the end of the publication.

- The Harvard system, in which each time a publication is referred to the author's name and year of publication are given; for example, "Further work (Jones 2001) has shown" or "Further work by Jones (2001) has shown". If there are two authors, both names are included. Where there are more than two authors, only the first name is quoted, followed by "*et al.*". The references are listed in full in alphabetical order of author names at the end of the publication.

There is no one standard way, however, of setting out a reference, whether obtained from a printed publication or from the Internet. This does not matter too much as long as sufficient information is included about each publication to allow it to be identified uniquely and traced. With references found on the Internet though, the date the information was accessed should also be included.

Books

References should include the author, title, publisher, year of publication, and preferably the town or city of publication, as below:

> Wharton, G. *Managing River Environments,* Cambridge, Cambridge University Press, 2000.

Where an author has contributed to a book which has been edited by a different author, details of both contributor and editor are included, for example:

> Xiong, D., "A three-stage computational approach to network matching", in Thill, J. C. (ed.), *Geographic Information Systems in Transportation Research*, Oxford, Pergamon, 2000, pp. 71–89.

Reports and theses are also referred to in a similar way. Usually reports are given code letters and numbers – in a format such as ST1/DOC/10/246 – as an identifier, and these should be included in the reference. References to theses should state the type of degree, such as MSc or PhD, and the institution where the work was carried out.

Conference proceedings

References to papers published in conference proceedings tend to be fairly long. To avoid confusing two conferences with similar names, it is important to include the number of the conference (if there is one) and the name and place it was held at, as shown below:

Kitchel, E., "The effects of blue light on ocular health", in *Vision Rehabilitation: Assessment, Intervention and Outcomes; selected papers from Vision '99: International Conference on Low Vision*, New York, July 1999. Lisse, Netherlands, Swets & Zeitlinger, 2000, pp. 81–83.

Patents

Every patent published is given a separate number, which should be included in the reference; for example:

Inventec Corp, *Telephone with Television Interface*, GB patent application 2344960A, 2000.

Standards

Standards are also published bearing individual numbers and codes, which should also be included in the reference; for example:

British Standards Institution, *Water Quality. Physical, Chemical and Biochemical Methods. Guidelines for selective immunoassays for the determination of plant treatment and pesticide agents*, 2000, BS 6068-2.69.

Printed journals

Because there are so many journals, each issue of which can contain a large number of papers, it is necessary to have a system by which each paper can be referred to precisely. This means including not only the author and title of the paper but also the name of the journal and details of which part or issue it appeared in, as in the reference below:

Watson, J. D. and Crick, F. H. C., "A structure for deoxyribose nucleic acid", *Nature*, **171**(4356), 1953, 737–738.

The volume number (the number given to all the separate issues published in any one year) usually appears in either italic or bold print. Titles of journals are printed in italic to distinguish them from the titles of papers. Journal titles are very frequently abbreviated, but unfortunately the recommended standard abbreviations are not always used.

If you are in doubt as to what an abbreviation stands for, it is better not to guess: a lot of time has been wasted chasing inaccurate references in this way. Abbreviations can be checked in several books, a recommended one being L.G. Alkire's *Periodical Title Abbreviations*, 12th edition, Detroit, Michigan, Gale Research, 2000.

Electronic journals

References to journals in electronic format should include the same information as their print-based equivalents, but with the indication that the publication is online, and a Web address.

> Chung, D. D. L., "Cement–matrix composites for smart structures". *Smart Materials and Structures* [online], 9(4), 2000, pp: 389 – 401. Available from: *http://www.iop.org* [Accessed: 9 February 2001].

World Wide Web (WWW)

The information given should include the author (whether personal or corporate), the year, title, place of publication, publisher, Uniform Resource Locator (URL) and date accessed.

> University of Washington. (1996). Template atlas of the primate brain [online]. Washington, US: University of Washington. Available from: *http://rprcsgi.rprc.washington.edu/~atlas/* [Accessed: 28 June 2000].

Personal email

If you include a reference to a personal email, it is important to obtain permission from the sender, which should appear first in the reference, followed by the sender's email address, date, subject, recipient and their email address.

> Lambert, J. (*J.Lambert@aston.ac.uk*). 7 August 2000. Re: *New database service.* Email to E. Smith (*Elizabeth_Smith@aston.ac.uk*).

Discussion lists

The information should include the name of the contributor, the date sent to the list, the title of the contribution, the name of the discussion list, the URL of list, and the date accessed.

> Abduh, M. 7 March 2000. Survey on utility of internet services for design-build projects. *Engineering integration* [online]. Available from: *engineering-integration@mailbase.ac.uk* [Accessed: 28 June 2000].

Chapter 2

Searching the Web

At the beginning of a new investigation, you will want to find as much information as possible about the topic. There are two reasons why it is best to do this in advance of practical or laboratory work. First, you are less likely to duplicate research, which has already been carried out elsewhere. Secondly, any information you find about existing work can be used as the starting-point for the new investigation. It is always tempting, particularly for new researchers, to put off this type of search and to begin experimentation immediately, but doing this can produce some unpleasant surprises later on.

Using previously known work

The easiest way of starting is to make use of any previously known work on the topic. If you are joining an established research group, there is almost certain to be one person with some knowledge of the topic who will be able to pass on at least a few references to relevant papers. In the introductions to these papers, the authors will have outlined and given references to previous work in the subject field. At least some of these references will be relevant to the topic and provide you with a good starting-point for your research. It is worth scanning these references to see if you can spot a review article. Not all reviews are named as such, so you need to look fairly carefully. Since reviews tend to be much longer than research papers, one clue to their presence is their length, indicated by the page numbering. Any article which includes the word "survey" in its title is also worth investigating. Following up these papers will produce a further set of references, some of which will probably be of use. Repeating this procedure once or twice should help you form an idea of the current stage of development in the subject.

It would be wrong, however, to give the impression that this type of search is sufficient by itself. Because the information has been collected in a fairly haphazard way, it is possible to miss important references. Also the search will not have picked up the very latest information: delays in publication plus the time required to prepare manuscripts mean that the most recent references included by authors will have appeared at least nine to 12 months previously.

What you need to do now is supplement this information by a more systematic search for information – the Internet, books, papers from journals, and patents if the subject has commercial or industrial potential. Knowing something about the subject field already will be a help in searching more selectively and efficiently.

Web sites

An obvious starting point is to look for a relevant Web site. As most people are aware, there is now a huge amount of information available on the Internet. Some of it is of good quality, giving information that would have taken days or weeks to obtain a few years ago. From the scientific, technical and medical angle, however, much is of it is of dubious value, particularly to the unwary.

Whether good, indifferent or poor, unless you have prior knowledge of a site, you will need to use a "discovery or search tool" of some kind. Although the names may vary, basically this comes down to using one of the following – a search engine, a classified directory or a subject gateway.

Search engines

When most people think of searching the Web for information, their starting point is likely to be one of the large search engines – *Altavista* (*http://uk.altavista.com/*), *Google* (*http://www.google.co.uk*), *Lycos* (*http://www.lycos.co.uk/*) and the like. A search engine – sometimes called a crawler, worm, robot or spider – is basically a piece of software, which trawls the Web looking for sites to include in its database. It operates by first identifying Web sites to be included in the database, secondly indexing some or all of the information in the pages, and thirdly by providing a searching mechanism and interface for people to use.

Though search engines are very easy to use, it is also very easy to be swamped by the information found, much of which is often only of fringe interest. In one survey only 18% of users claimed to always find the information they needed. Two-thirds of people admitted that they were often frustrated by Web searching. The following techniques are useful ways of improving on the results of searches.

- Try to be specific and use as many keywords as possible to describe the query. For example if you are looking for information on environmental problems with land re-use, use terms such as *contaminated land, land reclamation* or *brownfill sites,* rather than words such as *pollution* or *environment* or *land*, which will retrieve a huge number of sites. If you do not find very much using specific keywords, you can always broaden out the search and try again.

- Use the plus symbol "+" to link two or more keywords together. If for instance you were looking for information on the migration of the arctic tern, and typed in the search as *arctic tern migration*, then the search engine would normally look for documents containing any of these three words. Using the + symbol will instruct the search engine to look for the keywords on the same Web page. When the search was entered as *arctic tern navigation* on *Altavista*, over one million pages were found. When the search was repeated with the keywords linked as *+arctic +tern +migration*, a much more manageable 1500 or so pages were retrieved. (Make sure there is no space between the plus sign and the keyword, i.e. *+migration* not *+ migration*.)

- Enclose phrases in double quotation marks. What actually happens when double quotation marks are used is that the search engine looks for the two words adjacent to each other, a concept known as "proximity searching". For instance a search on *Google* for *ozone smogs* found over 600 sites. Repeating the search as *"ozone smogs"* brought up less than 30 sites.

- Exclude unwanted topics using the minus "-" symbol. For example if you were looking for information on waterborne pathogens, but did not want anything on the common bacterium *Escherichia coli*, you could enter the search as *waterborne pathogens -Escherichia coli*. The search engine would then look for pages containing the first keywords entered, then exclude any which also contained the keyword prefixed by the minus symbol. When this search was carried out on *Google, waterborne pathogens* retrieved over 10,000 sites. When the search was repeated as *waterborne pathogens -Escherichia coli*, fewer than two thousand sites were found. (Make sure that there is no space between the minus sign and the keyword, i.e. *- Escherichia coli*.)

- Try the more sophisticated retrieval features available on search engines. It should be possible to find a link on the opening Web page to these features, variously given names such as "advanced search", "advanced web search" or "power search". With the *Google* advanced search for example (Figure 4), the form can help users specify more exactly what information is required, and show how keywords should be linked. With many search engines, including *Alta Vista* and *Google*, keywords can also be linked together using the Boolean operators, "AND", "OR" and "NOT", outlined in Chapter 4.

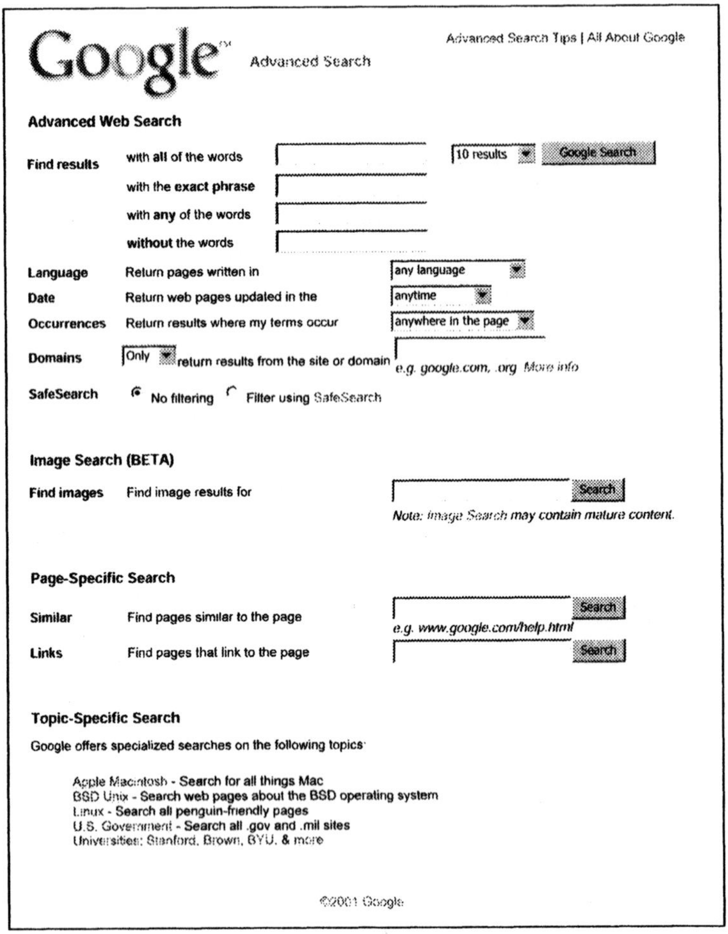

Figure 4: Google *advanced Web search. (The Google brand features are trademarks of Google, Inc.)*

Using these techniques should improve the relevance of the sites found. It is also worth checking the "help" or "search tips" link that should be displayed on the search engine's home page screen for more information on specific information retrieval features. No one search engine is comprehensive though; if you are not satisfied with the sites found, repeat the query on a different search engine.

Specialised search engines

As well as the large general search engines, there are some specialised ones which only look for Web sites in specific subject fields, particularly in the medical area.

A few examples include:

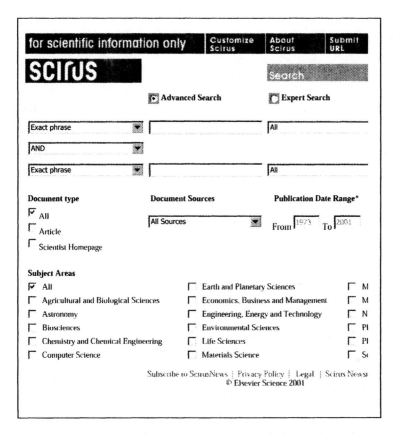

Figure 5: Scirus *advanced search (product of Elsevier Science)*

- *GlobalSpec (http://www.globalspec.com/home/)*, covering engineering components
- *MEDNETS (http://www.mednets.com/)*
- *Medical World Search (http://www.mwsearch.com/)*
- *Scirus (http://www.scirus.com/)*

The last of these search engines – *Scirus* – was launched by the scientific, technical and medical publisher Elsevier Science in 2001 (Figure 5). Elsevier's intention is that *Scirus* will concentrate only on sites with scientific content, such as university sites and authors Web pages, avoiding the general sites which can clutter up the results screens. It also includes both free and "access controlled sites" – Web services and databases for which a membership fee is required.

Metasearch engines

An additional option is to try a meta- or multisearch engine, such as *Ixquick* (*http://www.ixquick.com*) or *CNET Search.com* (*http://www.search.com/*). Metasearch engines work by searching a number of search engines at the same time, displaying the top hits from each. Using a metasearch engine can be an easy way of getting a bird's eye view of the information available. Searching on *Ixquick* for *waterborne pathogens* for instance found over 50 different Web sites, including an "Ask the experts" site from the journal *Scientific American* on effects of chlorine on bacteria in drinking water. One of the limitations of metasearch engines though is that advanced searching features, such as including phrases in quotations marks, may not be available. Another is that they may not include a "favourite" search engine – *Ixquick,* for example, did not cover *Google* when these searches were carried out.

Classified directories

In contrast to the automatic techniques used to construct the indexes of search engines, classified directories – often referred to as subject catalogues – are basically compiled by human beings. The Web sites may be chosen by a professional indexer, or picked out from requests to the directory by organisations, individuals and companies wanting to be included. Although *Yahoo* (*http://www.yahoo.com*) is the most well known, there are others, such as the *Dmoz Open Directory Project* (*http://dmoz.org*), the *Virtual Library* (*http://www.vlib.org*) and *BUBL LINK* (*http://www.bubl.ac.uk/link/*), shown in Figure 6. *BUBL* is an Internet-based reference service for the UK higher education community, with Web sites selected for their academic content. The "Link 5:15" displayed on screen refers to the fact that users can expect to find between five and 15 resources under each heading. Figure 7 shows some of the links listed on the Nanotechnology page in the Engineering and Technology Subject Category (not illustrated).

As the *BUBL* examples show, classified directories use a hierarchical, tree-like structure to organise the subject categories. Although it is usually possible to find Web sites on a directory just by typing in keywords, the tree structure is there to encourage easy browsing. This can be useful in the following circumstances:

- If it is proving difficult to find words to describe a topic. Information on the practical aspects of design of equipment, for example, can be hard to locate, but you can find Web sites on *Yahoo* by browsing the links from *Science* through to *Engineering*, to *Ergonomics*, and then *Bad Human Factors Design*. The last included an interesting site giving examples (with photographs) of designs – such as a kitchen timer and an ergonomically designed toothbrush – which are hard to use because they do not follow human factors principles.

Figure 6: BUBL LINK *selected internet resources*

BUBL LINK Catalogue of selected Internet resources

Home | Search | Subject Menus | A-Z | Dewey | Countries | Types | Updates | Random | About

620.5 Nanotechnology

Titles	Descriptions
1. Electronic Journals and Magazines on Molecular Nanotechnology	**Electronic Journals and Magazines on Molecular Nanotechnology**
2. Foresight Institute	Annotated links to 15 online journals and magazines about molecular modelling and nanotechnology.
3. Foresight Nanotechnology Publications	*Author:* Sean Morgan
4. Fractal Shape Changing Robots	*Subjects:* molecular modelling, nanotechnology
5. Introduction to Microengineering	*DeweyClass:* 620.5
6. Nanomedicine	*ResourceType:* journal index
7. Nanotechnology	*Location:* usa
8. Sandia MEMS Image Gallery	**Foresight Institute**
9. Sixth Foresight Conference on Molecular Nanotechnology	Aims to guide emerging technologies to improve the human condition, focusing on nanotechnology, the ability to build materials and products with atomic precision. Offers specialist and general articles on nanotechnology, and information on news, events and publications.

All links checked August 2001

Comments bubl@bubl.ac.uk

Electronic Journals and Magazines on Molecular Nanotechnology
Annotated links to 15 online journals and magazines about molecular modelling and nanotechnology.
Author: Sean Morgan
Subjects: molecular modelling, nanotechnology
DeweyClass: 620.5
ResourceType: journal index
Location: usa

Foresight Institute
Aims to guide emerging technologies to improve the human condition, focusing on nanotechnology, the ability to build materials and products with atomic precision. Offers specialist and general articles on nanotechnology, and information on news, events and publications.
Author: Foresight Institute
Subjects: nanotechnology
DeweyClass: 620.5
ResourceType: institution
Location: usa

Foresight Nanotechnology Publications
Quarterly newsletter intended to inform a wide audience about both technical and non-technical developments in nanotechnology, as well as background essays and briefing documents.
Author: Foresight Institute
Subjects: nanotechnology
DeweyClass: 620.5
ResourceType: magazine, documents
Location: usa

Fractal Shape Changing Robots
Illustrated speculation about the potential development and possibilities of nanotechnology.
Author: J Michael
Subjects: fractals, nanotechnology
DeweyClass: 620.5
ResourceType: documents
Location: uk

Introduction to Microengineering
Microengineering refers to the technologies and practice of making three-dimensional structures and devices with dimensions in the order of micrometers. This document introduces three of the micromachining techniques that are in use or under development: silicon micromachining, the Excimer laser and LIGA.
Author: Danny Banks
Subjects: manufacturing, nanotechnology
DeweyClass: 620.5
ResourceType: guide
Location: uk

Nanomedicine
Offers information on the potential of nanomedicine – the use of engineered nanodevices and nanostructures to monitor, repair, construct, or control human biological systems at a molecular level. Provides answers to frequently asked questions, technical papers on medical nanorobots

Figure 7: BUBL LINK *nanotechnology*

- If you want a broad overview of what is available in an area. While search engines are the best choice for specific queries, the classified directories are better at giving a big picture of a topic. For example someone looking for background on calibration and measurement can find a summary of the national and international organisations involved, on the *Dmoz Open Directory Project* following the links from *Science* through to *Technology* and then *Metrology*.

It is worth noting that what is being searched for in a directory are the subject categories, titles and descriptions of the Web sites. What is not being searched is an index built up from the full text of the Web pages themselves, as is the case with search engines. This being so, it is better to begin with broader keywords, working to the more specific as necessary.

Subject gateways and virtual libraries

Subject gateways – sometimes also called "virtual libraries" – are search tools which provide access to evaluated resources in specific disciplines. Superficially the impression is of a hybrid between a search engine and a classified directory – the gateways are organised in hierarchical structures for browsing, and usually have a search box for specific enquiries, but they are limited to specific subject fields and are relatively small in size.

Subject gateways have a lot to offer in the scientific, engineering and medical fields, particularly in the following circumstances:

- If you are seeking high-quality information – gateways only include resources that have been evaluated for their quality. The evaluation is likely to have been made by either information specialists or professionals from the subject field. Compared with search engines and classified directories, the number of sites catalogued is small – perhaps only 2,000 or so in some cases. The sites that are included are selected according to strict criteria based on their scope, accuracy, currency and ease of use.

- If you are only looking for information within a specific subject area or discipline, such as chemistry or engineering. For example *BIOME*, listed below, is a "hub" or group of five specialised biomedical gateways – *OMNI* (health and medicine), *VETGATE* (veterinary sciences), *BIORES* (biological research), *NATURAL* (natural world) and *AGRIFOR* (agriculture, food and forestry).

- If you are likely to be interested in mailing lists and usenet groups. Some subject gateways cover relevant lists and groups. *EEVL:* the Internet Guide to Engineering, Mathematics and Computing – for instance has an indexed archive to the last 40 days of articles

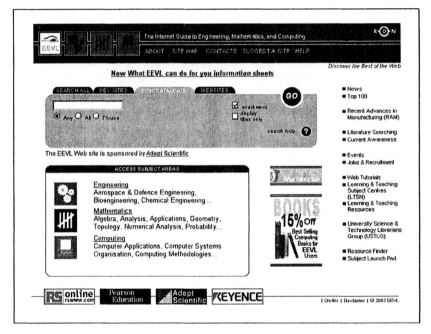

Figure 8: EEVL – the Internet Guide to Engineering, Mathematics and Computing

in Engineering Newsgroups (Figure 8). *Physicsweb*, listed below, also includes newsletters, mailing lists and usenet groups in the physical sciences fields.

Some of these gateways originate from commercial organisations, paid for by advertisements and sponsorship. Others such as *BIOME* and *EEVL* receive national funding – in the UK this has come from the Joint Information Systems Committee (JISC), a government-funded, strategic advisory committee for further and higher education.

Major gateways for the scientific, medical and engineering fields include:

- *AERADE (http://aerade.cranfield.ac.uk/)* – aerospace and defence information sources, run by Cranfield University and the Royal Military College at Shrivenham.

- *BIOME (http://biome.ac.uk/biome.html)* – based at the University of Nottingham. The BIOME gateways are aimed at researchers, students, lecturers, medics, veterinary surgeons, scientists and amateur enthusiasts in each of the subject fields covered.

- *BioMedNet (http://www.bmn.com/)* – owned by Elsevier Science. Its scope is wide and large scale – journals, books, research, jobs and products in the biological and medical subject fields.

- *Chemdex* (*http://www.chemdex.org*) – based at the University of Sheffield. A directory of evaluated scholarly resources for chemistry.
- *ChemSoc* (*http://www.chemsoc.org*) – the international chemistry societies network, hosted by the Royal Society of Chemistry (RSC). It includes education resources, jobs, forthcoming meetings and conferences, and a learning resources section for students and teachers of chemistry.
- *ChemWeb* (*http://www.chemweb.com*) – also owned by Elsevier Science, aimed at research and industrial chemists.
- *E4 Network* (*http://www.e4engineering.com/*) – a group of sites from the publisher of the *Engineer* magazine. The sites include an archive of engineering journals, jobs in the sector, subcontracting services, and technical specifications and data sheets (for which a subscription is required).
- *EEVL – the Internet Guide to Engineering, Mathematics and Computing* (*http://www.eevl.ac.uk*) based at Heriot-Watt University. As Figure 8 shows, EEVL provides links to a very large range of Web resources in engineering.
- *Eldis* (*http://www.ids.ac.uk/ids/info/index.html*) – information sources on development and the environment, hosted by the Institute of Development Studies at the University of Sussex.
- *iCrank.com* (*http://www.icrank.com*) – a gateway for mechanical engineers, including a directory of vendors, free trade magazines, design codes and specifications.
- *PhysicsWeb/TIPTOP* (*http://physicsweb.org/TIPTOP/*) – a large gateway run by the Institute of Physics, and including links to many of the pre-print servers mentioned in the previous chapter.
- *PSIgate* (*http://www.psigate.ac.uk/*) – high quality internet resources in the physical sciences.
- *Student Guide to Engineering Information Resources* (*http://www.helpengine.org*) – information and links to the major engineering institutions, centres and libraries in Britain, such as British Standards Institution, the Institute of Physics and the Department of the Environment, Transport and Regions. It also has practical hints and guidance for students on how to make effective use of the resources available.

Inevitably a list such as this will change over time. A good starting point for finding subject gateways is *PINAKES*, maintained by Heriot-Watt University at *http://www.hw.ac.uk/libWWW/irn/pinakes/pinakes.html*. Subtitled a "subject launchpad", this is a very useful Web page of logos and links to more than 40 academic and scholarly gateways. Heriot-Watt University also produce the *Internet Resources Newsletter* at *http://*

www.hw.ac.uk/libWWW/irn/irn.html. This newsletter, which is updated monthly, is a very useful way of keeping up to date with new, good Web sites in the scientific and technical fields.

Library Web pages

Another place you should look for useful Web sites is your own library or information service. Many services have set up their own subject specific guides or "pathfinders" to useful Web sites, such as the example shown in Figure 9. Library Web pages can be overlooked, but the sites included will have been carefully chosen by the staff to reflect the interests of the users of the service.

Evaluating Web sites

All searching involves evaluating the information found. The difference when searching for free Web sites on the Internet is that a higher level of caution is needed if you are to be sure that the information found is reliable and appropriate for your needs. Anyone is free to "publish" on the Internet. However unlike articles published in journals, no refereeing or peer review process will have taken place.

One technique for picking out winners is to ask the following questions :

- *Who — or which organisation – is responsible for the site?* This is important, because it will help in estimating how much authority you can place on the information found. For instance a search for information on ozone levels in the UK found – as would be expected – a large number of sites. The highest ranked ones included: a data compilation based on national air quality standards by a school in the Midlands; a UK government environment agency site presenting data collected between 1979 and 1998 at Lerwick in the Shetlands and Camborne in Cornwall; a Friends of the Earth smog briefing; a Green Party news report; and the UK government Met Office site. From the scientific point of view, the user needs to weigh up which sites are likely to provide authoritative, reliable data on the situation.

- *How accurate is the information likely to be?* For anyone new to a topic, accuracy is not an easy thing to judge. One thing you can do is to check if the sources of any factual information are clearly shown, and whether there are any references to published information, such as journal articles, which will have been refereed. If numerical data is included, look to see if the name of the source is given. If so it will help to make an assessment of how accurate

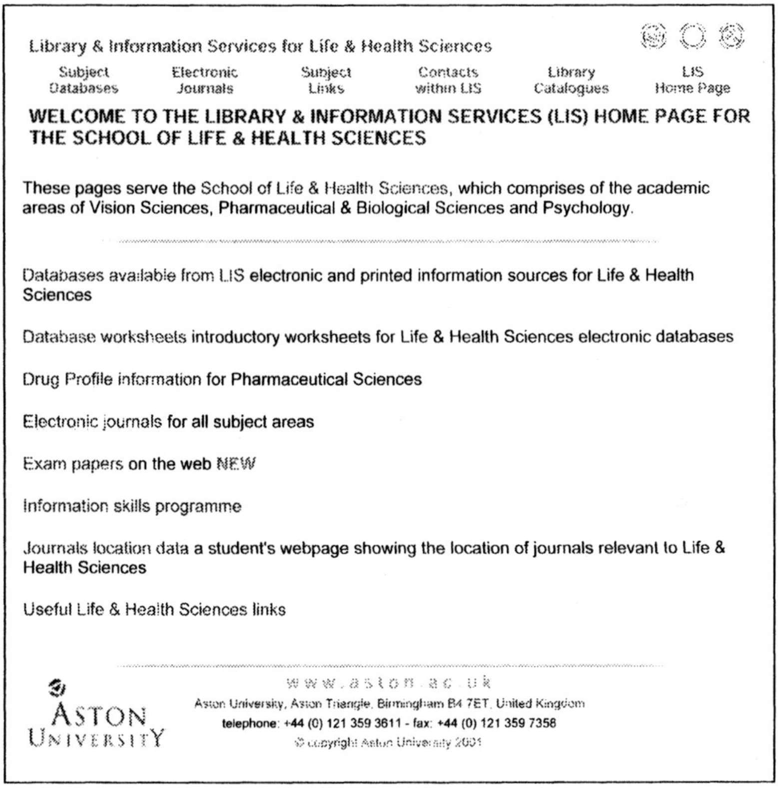

Library & Information Services for Life & Health Sciences

Subject Databases | Electronic Journals | Subject Links | Contacts within LIS | Library Catalogues | LIS Home Page

WELCOME TO THE LIBRARY & INFORMATION SERVICES (LIS) HOME PAGE FOR THE SCHOOL OF LIFE & HEALTH SCIENCES

These pages serve the School of Life & Health Sciences, which comprises of the academic areas of Vision Sciences, Pharmaceutical & Biological Sciences and Psychology.

Databases available from LIS electronic and printed information sources for Life & Health Sciences

Database worksheets introductory worksheets for Life & Health Sciences electronic databases

Drug Profile information for Pharmaceutical Sciences

Electronic journals for all subject areas

Exam papers on the web NEW

Information skills programme

Journals location data a student's webpage showing the location of journals relevant to Life & Health Sciences

Useful Life & Health Sciences links

ASTON UNIVERSITY

www.aston.ac.uk

Aston University, Aston Triangle, Birmingham B4 7ET, United Kingdom

telephone: +44 (0) 121 359 3611 - fax: +44 (0) 121 359 7358

© copyright Aston University 2001

Figure 9: Library Web page

the data is likely to be. Other basic points are to look at whether there are any spelling or grammatical mistakes, as these could indicate a lack of care in putting the site together.

- *Why was the site made available?* This is important because of the need to consider whether the information is likely to be biased in any way. Again this is connected with who produced the site, and whether this is likely to have influenced the way the data is presented. In a search, for example, on the effectiveness of the drug Ritalin on the syndrome attention-deficit hyperactivity disorder (ADHD) in children, the sites found included the following: an advertisement for treatment of ADHD; a guide to best practice on ADHD in children for psychologists, written by a national professional psychological society; a paper by a university student; and an article on drugged obedience in schools by a "personologist" specialising in coaching children and parents in the practical ways of decreasing conflict and increasing co-operation. It would be reasonable to assume a high level of objectivity from the report by the professional psychological society, which has a reputation to protect. The advertisement for ADHD on the other hand is putting forward a particular perspective, which may – or may not – be biased in any way.

- *How comprehensive is the information?* You need to try to gauge how broad or deep the coverage of the topic is. If there is a site map this can give a useful impression of the coverage. The number of links to other sites is another clue as to how much thought the site's creators have given to its comprehensiveness.

- *How current is the information?* The level of importance placed on this depends on the subject. With a rapidly developing area such as the spread of multidrug-resistant bacteria – the so-called "superbugs" – in hospitals, it would be vital to make certain the information is recent. There is no guarantee, of course, that if a Web site is regularly updated that the information you want is actually current. However, using a Web site that has not been revised for several months gives an indication that the person or organisation involved in its production does not give it the highest of priorities.

It is worth looking for links such as "About", "Frequently Asked Questions", or "News" when evaluating a Web site. These links are a good means of finding out who has put the site together, and can help to evaluate the information found in terms of its accuracy, reliability, objectivity and currency. If you cannot easily discover the provenance or origin of the site – a fairly common occurrence – treat the information found with great caution.

Summary

- Find out as much as possible about the subject by following up the references in any papers or books in your possession.

- Reduce the amount of information of fringe interest when searching the Web by using the "+", "-" symbols and double quotation marks, or the advanced features provided by search engines.

- Try the classified directories and subject gateways to find Web sites that have been subjected to an external assessment for quality and relevance.

- Remember to evaluate the quality of any information you find on free Web sites.

- If you want to improve your Web searching, try the *RDN (Resource Discovery Network) Virtual Training Suite* at *http://www.vts.rdn.ac.uk/*. This is a set of free Web-based tutorials aimed at helping students, lecturers and researchers find good-quality Internet sites in their subject fields. There are tutorials for medics, chemists, earth scientists, physicists, mathematicians, vets, agriculturists, bio-researchers, environmentalists and engineers.

Chapter 3

Using libraries

Although the starting point when searching for information may now be the Web, libraries remain a vital source of information. Before outlining how you can use library facilities to find information, there are a couple of points worth mentioning. The first is that we have concentrated on outlining the general principles of searching, illustrating these with examples from some major information sources. There are many more potential information sources which could not be included: your library or information centre will know of these sources and be able to give good advice on the best ones to use. Be prepared to ask, the staff will be only too willing to help. The second point is that there is really no one single right way of searching for information, but a number of different methods, one or more of which will, it is hoped, produce results. What we aim to do is to point you in the right direction.

Encyclopaedias, handbooks and guides to the literature

A traditional route when searching for information is to look for an encyclopaedia which covers the discipline. There are some useful encyclopaedias freely available via the Web. One to try is *Bartleby.com* (*http://www.bartleby.com/65*). In addition to the general encyclopaedias, there are also some which specialise in covering scientific fields – another available free via the Web is the *ADAM Medical Encyclopaedia (MEDLINE Plus)* at *http://www.nlm.nih.gov/medlineplus/encyclopedia.html*.

In engineering too there are many printed handbooks, such as *Kempe's Engineers Year-book* shown in Figure 10, which are good sources of practical information. Enyclopaedias and handbooks are not intended just for the layman or amateur. They are generally written by experts in a subject and, though the articles themselves tend to be fairly terse and to the point, references are usually included to some of the key works in a subject field for further reading.

Solar energy

By Professor T Muneer, PhD, CEng, MIMechE, FCIBSE

Solar radiation and daylight are essential to life on Earth. Solar radiation affects the Earth's weather processes which determine the natural environment. Its presence at the Earth's surface is necessary for the provision of food for mankind. Thus it is important to be able to understand the physics of solar radiation and daylight. Understanding of the climatological study of radiation is comparatively new. Until 1960 there were only three stations in north-west Europe with irradiation records exceeding a 25 year period. During 1991, in response to a call made by Commission Internationale de l'Eclairage (CIE), an international measurement programme for daylight and solar radiation was initiated.

TERMINOLOGY

Solar radiation (W/m^2) or **luminance** (candela/m^2) refer to the energy emanating from the Sun.

Luminance is the energy contained within the visible part of the solar radiation spectrum (0·39 to 0·78 μm).

Irradiation (Wh/m^2 or J/m^2) and **illumination** (lumen-hour/m^2) refer to the cumulative energy incident on a surface in a given period of time.

Irradiance (W/m^2) and **illuminance** (lux) refer to the instantaneous incident energy.

Insolation is synonymous with **solar irradiation**.

The interception of solar radiation by a surface is a function of that surface's geometry, and determines their microclimatic interaction, ie the energy exchange between the surface and its surroundings. Irradiation available at arbitrarily sloped surfaces is a prerequisite in many sciences. For example, agricultural meteorology, photobiology, animal husbandry, daylighting, comfort air-conditioning, building sciences and solar energy utilisation, all require an estimation of the availability of energy on slopes.

The Kyoto Protocol on global warming has been used as a challenge to building services engineers to get involved in a CO_2 permit scheme (ref 1). Solar energy may be considered a serious candidate for reducing the use of fossil fuels in buildings. In fact, the annual energy incident on UK buildings (1614 TWh) exceeds the country's oil production (1504 TWh). Whereas the UK electricity consumption is 300 TWh the potential for solar electrical generation is 200 TWh (ref 2). Making best use of daylight (eg with design elements such as atria, sloping facades and large windows can produce significant savings. Research has shown that savings of 20 to 40% are attainable by utilising daylight effectively due to the increased contribution of daylight results in lower sensible heat gains. This has the knock-on effect of lowering the cooling requirements of the buildings' air conditioning.

The ever-falling prices and increasing processing power of personal computers have led to a significantly increased sophistication in building energy analysis. A study by the US-based Semiconductor Industry Association (ref 3) has shown that by the year 2001 integrated circuits of 256 MB RAM will be commonly available, such that computers would use detailed databases of solar radiation, daylight illuminance and other weather parameters. Towards this end, the present chapter provides information on the relevant models and reviews the state-of-the-art techniques now available. Recent developments in solar energy utilisation technology are also presented. Thus, there are sections on solar radiation and daylight as well as solar collectors, solar heating and photovoltaic systems. Wherever possible information is given via mathematical relationships, graphics and in a tabular form, so that the reader may incorporate them easily into computer programming or spreadsheet packages.

SOLAR RADIATION AND DAYLIGHT

Solar day. A solar day is defined to be the interval of time from the moment the sun crosses the local meridian to the next time it crosses the same meridian. Owing to the fact that the earth rotates in a diurnal cycle as well as moves forward in its orbit, the time required for one full rotation of the earth is less than a solar day by about 4 minutes.

In many solar energy applications one needs to calculate the day number (DN) corresponding to a given date. In a given year, DN is defined as the number of days elapsed since the start of the year up to a given date.

Equation of time (EOT). The solar day defined above varies in length throughout the year due to:

1. the tilt of the earth's axis with respect to the plane of the ecliptic containing the respective centres of the sun and the earth; and,
2. the angle swept out by the earth-sun vector during any given period of time, which depends upon the earth's position in its orbit.

Figure 10: Kempe's Engineers Year-book

Another good way for newcomers to a subject to orient themselves is to find a relevant guide to information in their subject field. They range in size from a few Web pages to substantial books, depending on their origin and subject, but they all have the same basic purpose – to help you find out what has been published in the subject. The benefit of using these guides is that they give a good grounding in the literature of a subject, which can then be supplemented if necessary with more recent information.

Library catalogues

Most library catalogues are now computerised, with the library's stock recorded in an online database. Online catalogues sited within library buildings often have "proprietary" interfaces, with the layout of the information on the screen being determined by the type of library management software used to create the database of stock records. However, many library catalogues can now be searched using the WWW, with the advantage that the screen display looks similar to any other Web-based service, enabling access from anyone working in laboratories, offices or from home.

Searching by author and title

All library catalogues have the same basic function – to let you find out if a book or journal you want is in a library. To do this, a catalogue displays in alphabetical order the names of the authors and editors of books in stock along with the associated information about title, edition, publisher, year of publication and classification number. Most catalogues also display the titles of books separately, so that if you only know the title of the book you can still find out if it is in stock. With common surnames such as Smith, Williams, Brown and so on, it can be quicker to search for a book by its title than by its author.

Every book in a library is given a classification number or code, which represents the subject. Several different schemes have been devised for the classification of books – the commonest, and the one found in most public and many academic libraries, is the Dewey Decimal Classification. In this system, general subject fields are represented by a three-figure classification number, with books on organic chemistry, for example, being given the number 547. Specialised subject fields are represented by longer numbers, so that a book on polymer science, a branch of organic chemistry, would be given the number 547.84. Books are arranged on the shelves in classification number or code order – it is obviously necessary to find what classification number has been given to the book you want before looking for it on the shelves.

With an online or Web catalogue the system will prompt you to enter the information needed. The computer matches this with the records in the database, and a list of the most closely related items is displayed on screen, linking through to a record of each item, as illustrated in Figure 11. The details included in this record are fairly typical – the name, title, edition and publisher of the book, and the class number, and whether the item is in stock or on loan to someone else. The three letter code following the class number – STA in the example – is taken from the author's name (or if there is no author or editor, then the title). It is used as a means of filing books allocated the same classification number on the shelves.

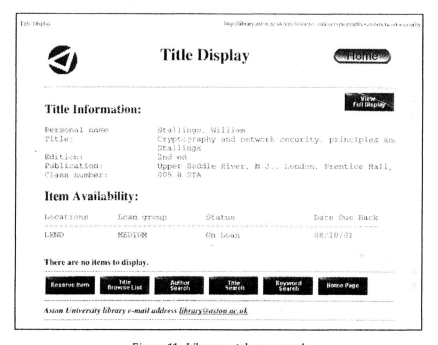

Figure 11: Library catalogue record

A catalogue record should also give the International Standard Book Number (ISBN), a unique identifying number given to each book title at the time of publication. In addition, most libraries allocate another specific number to each copy of each book in stock. This control or barcode number (there is some variation in the names used) is used to keep track of the whereabouts of each book in the library – whether it is on loan, on the shelves, or in a reservations section waiting to be collected by a reader. In the example shown, the button "view full display" links through to these details.

There are two points worth noting about the way names and titles are displayed in catalogues. The first, fairly obvious, one is that initial articles such as "the", "an" and "a" are ignored for filing purposes. *The Concise Oxford*

Dictionary, for example, will be listed under "*Concise ...*". Perhaps less obvious but important is the fact that words and phrases can be arranged by two different methods: letter by letter or word by word. With the letter by letter method, the spaces between the words are disregarded, whereas in the word by word method, the spaces between words are significant.

The different results produced by the two methods can be seen below.

letter by letter	*word by word*
database	data compression
database management systems	data transmission
databases	database
data compression	database management systems
data transmission	

Searching by keyword

If you do not know the names of any authors or titles in the subject field, how can you find out if the library has any relevant books? The obvious thing to do is to walk round the shelves until you find the right place. If the library or information centre is well signposted, this approach can be effective in finding general books in big subject fields such as electronic engineering or organic chemistry. However,it is not an effective way of finding books on specialised topics which, because there are so many, cannot be so clearly labelled.

A better option is to use the "keyword search" which most computerised catalogues provide, with the system matching the word(s) input with all the titles in the catalogue. Keyword searching has the advantage, as Figure 12 shows, that the search is not just limited to books with the keywords at the beginning of the title. This search – for books about network security – as well as finding titles such as *Network and internet network security,* also retrieved *Secrets and lies* and *Maximum security,* where the keywords "network security" are part of the subtitles of the books.

This approach also means you can be more certain of having found all the books in your library on a topic. It is impossible to be sure, just by checking the shelves at the right classification number, that you have found all the relevant books. Some will have been borrowed by other readers, others will be missing because they are reserved, and a few may be waiting to be re-shelved or repaired. Although you might not have instant access to the books as they may be on loan, anything that looks interesting could be reserved so that it can be saved for you on return.

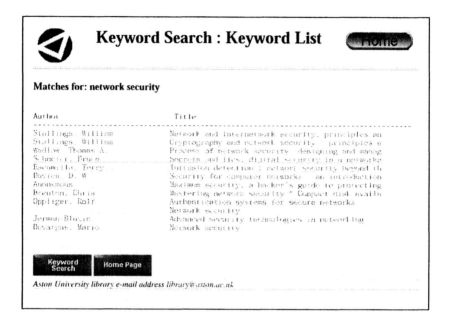

Figure 12: Keyword search

Other subject searching techniques
Although keyword searching is the most common and popular way of looking for books on specific subjects, many library catalogues provide other techniques which can be used.

- One approach is to link subjects to specific books, as shown below. The numbers indicate how many books the library has on the topic, and link through to the specific items:

    Visible and ultraviolet spectroscopy (8)

    VISICALC computer program (6)

    Vision (7)

    Vision disorders (5)

    Vision: photography (9)

    Visual aids (2)

- Another technique is to provide an alphabetical subject index, bringing together different aspects of a field or discipline. When a word or phrase is entered, the catalogue displays a list, with classification numbers for the subjects, as follows:

Optical Metrology: Optics	535.8
Optical Microscopy: Biology	578.4

Optical Pattern Recognition: Computer Systems 006.42

Optical Pattern Recognition: Electrical Engineering 621.380414

Optical Waveguides: Electrical Engineering 621.380414

Optical Waveguides: Optics 535.89

- A third technique is to provide a record of all books in a library in order by their classification numbers, so that all books on the same subject are together. To see a list of books on a subject you need to key in the appropriate classification number, as illustrated:

550.1	Geologic Time	Elcher
550.1	Geological Time	Kirkaldy
550.1	How Old is the Earth	Hurley
550.12	Geological Maps	Simpson
550.2	Space Geology	King

Libraries do not all use the same software packages for their catalogues. Although all should be able to be used for subject searching, the options available and the names do vary to some extent. Some catalogues have more advanced search features available, which make it feasible to specify how keywords should be combined together, so that for example you could search for books on bacteria OR viruses, or bacteria NOT pathogenic. The main point is to be aware that these different options exist, and to explore the ones available that may be useful to you.

Searching for journals

With some library catalogues it is possible to limit a search to journal titles only, so that if you are looking for the journal *New Civil Engineer*, for instance, it might be displayed as follows:

New Civil Engineer

New Covenant Record

New Edinburgh Review

New England Business Record

Other catalogues do not provide an option to differentiate between the titles of journals and books, so that the *New Civil Engineer* could be displayed along with similar alphabetical titles of books as follows:

New Civil Engineer

New Civil Engineer Consultants File

New Class, an analysis of the Communist System

Whatever the display, for a printed journal there should be a record of each journal name, plus details of the years in stock, and the shelf mark or location. An example of how this information might be shown is given below:

Title:	New Civil Engineer
Publication:	EMAP Readerlink
Class Number:	621C New
Holdings:	1978–
Location:	Per

Libraries do not always take a journal from the very first part or issue; very often a subscription may not start until after a journal has been in existence for some years. In this case the holdings – the years of the publication in stock — start in 1978. You need to check the date of your journal reference with the year and volume number – if available – to make sure it is in the library. If a journal subscription is subsequently cancelled, then the holdings should show the closure date, such as Vol 1–238, 1964–2000.

If the journal is in stock as printed copies, the location will be displayed in the catalogue, so you can find it on the shelves. The situation with journals published in electronic format is slightly more complicated. Some libraries include all the titles of the electronic journals to which they subscribe in their catalogue, making this a "one-stop shop" for checking purposes. Other libraries keep the list of electronic journals separate from the catalogue. What this means in practice is that it may be necessary to make two checks – the main library catalogue and the separate list of electronic journals – to be certain whether or not a title is available.

If electronic journals are included in the library catalogue, there may be a direct hyperlink to the title concerned, so that you can click on this to get to the Web site immediately, as in the example below:

Title:	International journal of pharmaceutics
Publication:	Elsevier
Internet Resource:	Science direct electronic journals
Class number:	615 INT
Location:	ScienceDirect

If not, it will be necessary to record the Web address and access the site on a different workstation. Although this may be irritating, there is a sound reason for the practice – with a limited number of workstations available, a library cannot afford to have the terminals occupied for long spells of time by users surfing the Internet, while other users are waiting to search the catalogue. More information about accessing electronic journals is given in Chapter 5.

Databases of published books

It is unlikely that you would find every relevant book on your topic in a library or information centre. There will probably be books that you know of which have not been bought by the library. These can be borrowed for you by a procedure known as interlibrary loan, described in Chapter 5. Almost certainly there will also have been other relevant books published, which you do not know about and which are not in your library. If you have not found very much, you will probably need to extend your search by using a database of published books. With the advantage of having some background knowledge, you can adopt a fairly selective approach which will prevent you being overwhelmed with seemingly relevant material.

The Web-based bookshops – such as *Amazon* (*http://www.amazon.co.uk*), *Bol* (*http://www.bol.com*), *Blackwell* (*http://www.bookshop.blackwell.co.uk*) and *Bibliofind* (*http://www.bibliofind.com*) – would probably be most people's first choice here. With the exception of *Bibliofind*, which specialises in rare and second-hand books, in the main the titles found will be those that are in print, i.e. copies can be bought from the publishers. Since most books tend to stay in print for only a few years, the majority of the titles included will be fairly recent. Older books are likely to be those which have proved to be of permanent value, and have been reprinted when all the original copies have been sold. For someone working in a rapidly changing subject field or one where there have been many recent developments – genetic engineering and information technology being obvious examples – this could be sufficient.

Other library catalogues

For many subject fields, though, it could well be useful to get an overview of what has been published over the last 20 or 30 years. Recent developments in large-scale, online library catalogues – freely accessible over the Web – have made this type of searching much easier. A good place to start is the *COPAC* catalogue, at *http://copac.ac.uk/copac/*. *COPAC* is a union catalogue of the stock of over 20 university libraries in the UK – Imperial College of Science, Technology and Medicine, Oxford, Cambridge, Glasgow and Edinburgh are just some of the contributing organisations. The *COPAC* home page and the results of a

COPAC provides *FREE access* to the merged online catalogues of 20 of the largest university research libraries in the UK and Ireland.

About COPAC
Libraries
Userguider
FAQ page
User Support
Z39.50 access
Related Links
Feedback

To Start a COPAC search session select **Enter COPAC** below.

🛈 **NEWS: Edinburgh circulation data now available**
Real-time circulation data is now available for documents held by the University of Edinburgh. This means that when you view the Edinburgh Holdings Display for a document you can see how many copies there are, whether they are currently on-loan, and if so, when they are due back. This circulation data is now available for 12 libraries, and we hope more will be included in the near future. (13th September 2001)
(More on local holdings in the 2000 news archive)

NEWS: Imperial catalogue reload complete
We have finished reloading the catalogue of the Imperial College of Science, Technology and Medicine. This was necessitated by a change in their local library system, with associated changes to their records. (Updated - 12th September 2001)

[News Archive]

For Information and Advice please read our FAQ page or contact the COPAC Helpdesk

COPAC is one of the MIMAS services, produced at Manchester Computing, University of Manchester. COPAC is funded by JISC and uses records supplied by CURL.

COPAC is a trademark of the Victoria University of Manchester

Figure 13: COPAC *home page*

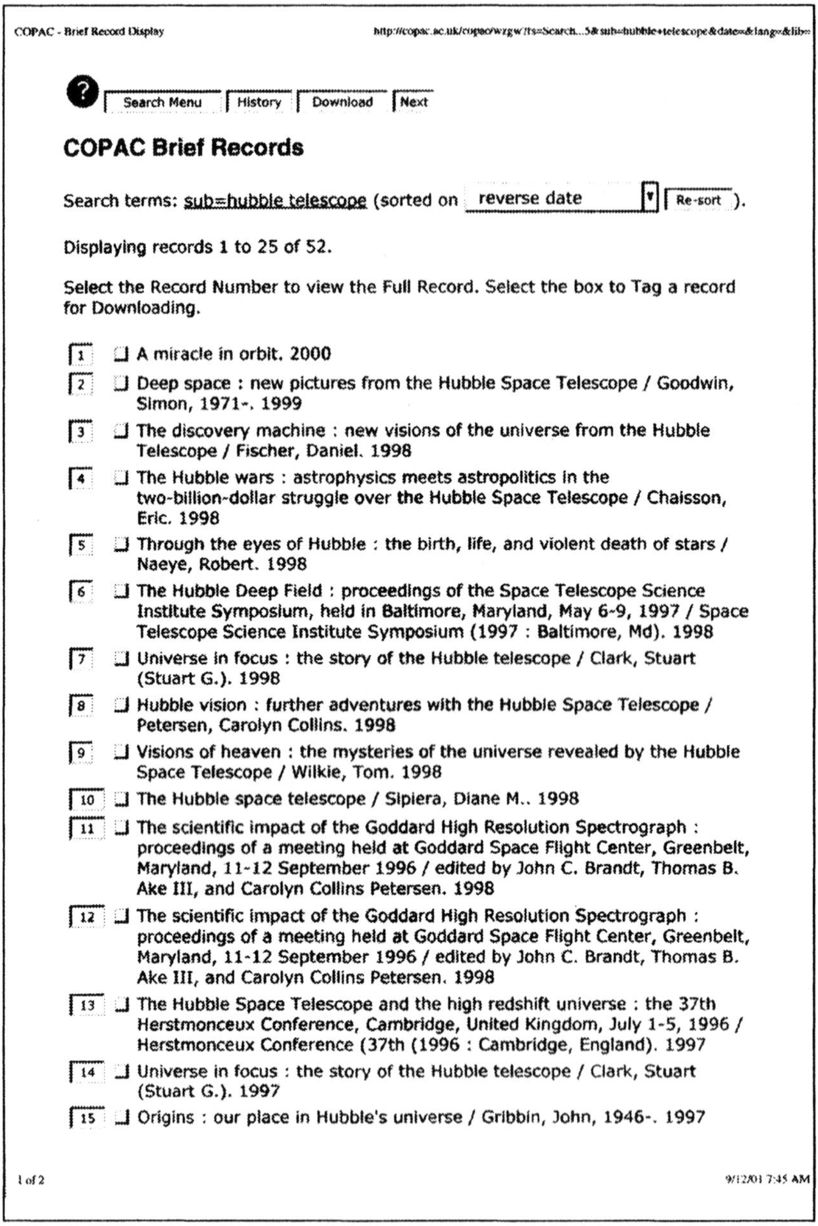

COPAC - Brief Record Display   http://copac.ac.uk/copao/wzgw/?ts=Search...5&sub=hubble+telescope&date=&lang=&lib=

? | Search Menu | History | Download | Next |

COPAC Brief Records

Search terms: <u>sub=hubble telescope</u> (sorted on | reverse date | ▼ | | Re-sort |).

Displaying records 1 to 25 of 52.

Select the Record Number to view the Full Record. Select the box to Tag a record for Downloading.

| 1 | ▢ A miracle in orbit. 2000

| 2 | ▢ Deep space : new pictures from the Hubble Space Telescope / Goodwin, Simon, 1971-. 1999

| 3 | ▢ The discovery machine : new visions of the universe from the Hubble Telescope / Fischer, Daniel. 1998

| 4 | ▢ The Hubble wars : astrophysics meets astropolitics in the two-billion-dollar struggle over the Hubble Space Telescope / Chaisson, Eric. 1998

| 5 | ▢ Through the eyes of Hubble : the birth, life, and violent death of stars / Naeye, Robert. 1998

| 6 | ▢ The Hubble Deep Field : proceedings of the Space Telescope Science Institute Symposium, held in Baltimore, Maryland, May 6-9, 1997 / Space Telescope Science Institute Symposium (1997 : Baltimore, Md). 1998

| 7 | ▢ Universe in focus : the story of the Hubble telescope / Clark, Stuart (Stuart G.). 1998

| 8 | ▢ Hubble vision : further adventures with the Hubble Space Telescope / Petersen, Carolyn Collins. 1998

| 9 | ▢ Visions of heaven : the mysteries of the universe revealed by the Hubble Space Telescope / Wilkie, Tom. 1998

| 10 | ▢ The Hubble space telescope / Sipiera, Diane M.. 1998

| 11 | ▢ The scientific impact of the Goddard High Resolution Spectrograph : proceedings of a meeting held at Goddard Space Flight Center, Greenbelt, Maryland, 11-12 September 1996 / edited by John C. Brandt, Thomas B. Ake III, and Carolyn Collins Petersen. 1998

| 12 | ▢ The scientific impact of the Goddard High Resolution Spectrograph : proceedings of a meeting held at Goddard Space Flight Center, Greenbelt, Maryland, 11-12 September 1996 / edited by John C. Brandt, Thomas B. Ake III, and Carolyn Collins Petersen. 1998

| 13 | ▢ The Hubble Space Telescope and the high redshift universe : the 37th Herstmonceux Conference, Cambridge, United Kingdom, July 1-5, 1996 / Herstmonceux Conference (37th (1996 : Cambridge, England). 1997

| 14 | ▢ Universe in focus : the story of the Hubble telescope / Clark, Stuart (Stuart G.). 1997

| 15 | ▢ Origins : our place in Hubble's universe / Gribbin, John, 1946-. 1997

1 of 2   9/12/01 7:45 AM

Figure 14: COPAC search results

search for books on the Hubble telescope are shown in Figures 13 and 14.

Another very useful source is *BLPC – the British Library Public Catalogue* at http://blpc.bl.uk/. This Web site is the starting point for searching the stock of the British Library, some of which dates back more than 250 years. One of the main benefits of searching *COPAC* and *BLPC* is that you are much more likely to come across the hard-to-find literature. Both have wide coverage of conference proceedings, reports from professional societies, national and international bodies for instance the World Health Organization, and publications from UK government agencies, such as the Department for Environment, Food and Rural Affairs, or the Advisory Committee on Dangerous Pathogens.

Try to keep a record of all essential information of any books, conference proceedings or other items that you find useful. It is very easy, especially if you are in a hurry, to jot down minimum details, but it can lead to confusion later. There are for instance over 450 books and conference proceedings with the keywords *biological chemistry* in their title listed on *COPAC*, so identifying the one needed just from the title could take a long time. If you want to ask your library to buy a copy of the book or borrow it from elsewhere, you will need to know the author, title and either the publisher or year of publication. If you then later want to refer to the book in an article, all these details plus the place of publication will be needed.

Theses

Mention has already been made of the literature survey and review included in every thesis or dissertation. You can find details of some theses in the *COPAC* union catalogue, but there are more specialised tools available for this purpose. The best source of information on theses published in Great Britain and Ireland is *Index to Theses*, published both in print and on the Web by Expert Information. Unlike the other Web sites mentioned in this chapter, *Index to Theses* is subscription based, i.e. an organisation has to pay an annual fee to use the information, so you would need to check with your library or information service to see if access is available. The Web site provides four search options – Quick, Simple, Standard and Advanced – and a mechanism for finding research carried out at a particular university or during a specific period of time. An example of a search for theses on the transmission of tuberculosis,

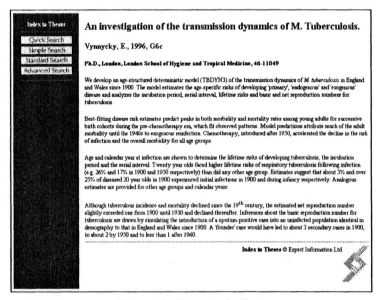

Figure 15: Index to Theses simple search.
(Reproduced with permission from: Index to theses
www.theses.com, [/]Expert Information.)*

An investigation of the transmission dynamics of M. Tuberculosis.

Vynnycky, E., 1996, G6c

Ph.D., London, London School of Hygiene and Tropical Medicine, 46-11049

We develop an age-structured deterministic model (TBDYN3) of the transmission dynamics of *M. tuberculosis* in England and Wales since 1900. The model estimates the age-specific risks of developing 'primary', 'endogenous' and 'exogenous' disease and analyzes the incubation period, serial interval, lifetime risks and basic and net reproduction numbers for tuberculosis.

Best-fitting disease risk estimates predict peaks in both morbidity and mortality rates among young adults for successive birth cohorts during the pre-chemotherapy era, which fit observed patterns. Model predictions attribute much of the adult morbidity until the 1940s to exogenous reinfection. Chemotherapy, introduced after 1950, accelerated the decline in the risk of infection and the overall morbidity for all age groups.

Age and calendar year at infection are shown to determine the lifetime risks of developing tuberculosis, the incubation period and the serial interval. Twenty year olds faced higher lifetime risks of respiratory tuberculosis following infection (e.g. 26% and 17% in 1900 and 1950 respectively) than did any other age group. Estimates suggest that about 3% and over 25% of diseased 20 year olds in 1900 experienced initial infections in 1900 and during infancy respectively. Analogous estimates are provided for other age groups and calendar years.

Although tuberculous incidence and mortality declined since the 19th century, the estimated net reproduction number slightly exceeded one from 1900 until 1930 and declined thereafter. Inferences about the basic reproduction number for tuberculosis are drawn by simulating the introduction of a sputum-positive case into an uninfected population identical in demography to that in England and Wales since 1900. A 'founder' case would have led to about 3 secondary cases in 1900, to about 2 by 1950 and to less than 1 after 1960.

Index to Theses © Expert Information Ltd

Figure 16: Abstract of a thesis.
(Reproduced with permission from: Index to Theses
www.theses.com, [/]Expert Information.)*

and an abstract of one of the documents found are shown in Figures 15 and 16 .

Quite heavy use is made of the *Index to Theses* by people who have heard of work carried out at a particular institution. Although they usually know roughly when the research was carried out, they sometimes have difficulties in finding the actual thesis. This is because there have been delays in the past between the submission of a thesis and its appearance in the index. Because of this it is a good idea when looking for an older thesis to check back through several years around about the expected date of submission.

Most US and Canadian theses can be found in *Digital Dissertations*, published by UMI ProQuest (*http://wwwlib.umi.com/dissertations/*). The most recent two years are available free, but to search the complete database – which goes as far back as 1861– your organisation will need to have paid for a subscription. Although this might seem a deterrent, do not be put off – the staff in your library or information unit will have arranged subscriptions to services relevant to your organisation, so do ask for details of the ones available to you.

Summary

- Try encyclopaedias and handbooks if you need authoritative information as background on a new topic.

- Be aware of the different search options available via your library catalogue – not all work in the same way.

- Use *COPAC* or the *British Library Public Catalogue* to find other relevant books, conference proceedings and government publications, and national and international reports.

- Do not overlook theses, both for their value as state-of-the-art reviews, and to ensure that you do not repeat work already carried out elsewhere.

Chapter 4

Using bibliographic databases

The importance of bibliographic or indexing and abstracting databases in making the information contained in journals, conference proceedings and reports more accessible has already been mentioned in Chapter 1. Some of today's leading bibliographic databases started out as printed publications over a hundred years ago as a means of bringing order and control to the burgeoning literature of science, technology and medicine. Most bibliographic databases can now be searched using the Web, but there are some that are produced and sold as CD-ROMs, and a few are still available only in printed format. Whatever the format, however, it is useful to have some knowledge of the structure and indexing techniques used by these databases.

Structure

The basic units of all bibliographic databases, whatever the subject field, are descriptions or "bibliographies" of publications – hence the name. In a few databases, these descriptions only consist of references or citations to journal articles, conference proceedings, patents and so on. Most also include summaries or abstracts of the information contained, which is obviously an advantage in deciding if the complete item is likely to be relevant or not. With some bibliographic databases, the abstracts are quite lengthy, giving information about experimental methods as well as conclusions. With others the abstracts are much briefer, only indicating the main findings.

A sample record from the *MEDLINE* database, produced by the National Library of Medicine (NLM) in the United States is shown in Figure 17. *MEDLINE* is a very large, long-established bibliographic database, covering the subject fields of medicine, nursing, veterinary medicine, health care and pre-clinical sciences. Setting aside for the time being the information and boxes at the top and side of the screen display, it can be seen that the record consists of a number of separate parts or fields:

- the abbreviated title of the journal and reference
- the title of the article
- the authors
- their place of work

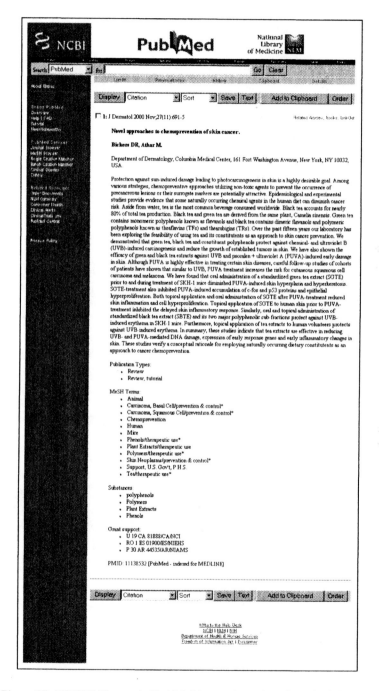

Figure 17: MEDLINE record. (PubMed is a registered trademark of the US National Library of Medicine.)

- the abstract
- the type of publication – in this case a review
- the *MeSH* (*Medical Subject Headings*) terms, which are keywords describing the subject field allocated to the article by professional indexers
- substances – the names of chemicals discussed in the article
- a reference number relating to the grant-awarding body which funded the research project
- a unique identification number

Not all records from bibliographic databases follow the same format as *MEDLINE* – there is a wide variation in the use of fields, such as "publication types" and the way subject indexing keywords are allocated to records. As a comparison, look at the layout of the information in Figure 18, a record from the *INSPEC* database which covers computing, information technology, physics, electrical, electronic and control engineering. However the main fields – the authors, the title of the paper, the name and reference of the journal or conference proceedings – will always be present.

Indexing

To make the records in a database searchable, the information contained must be indexed. There are variations in the way different database producers – or suppliers as they are sometimes called – index their particular product, but the underlying processes are similar. Although it is feasible to use these databases without any knowledge of these processes, knowing something about how databases are constructed will help you to carry out better searches in the long term.

In general terms, the procedure involves taking all the useful words from a field or part of a record, and storing them in an index belonging to that field, a process carried out by computerised techniques. In the *MEDLINE* database for example, the names, *D. R. Bickers* and *M. Athar* would be extracted from the record shown and added to the author index. Similarly the words in the abstract, such as *protection*, *damage* and *photocarcinogenesis*, will also be automatically extracted and placed in a subject index of abstract keywords. Every record inevitably includes so-called trivial words such as *of*, *is* and *the*. The software which carries out the automatic analysis procedure is programmed to exclude these non-meaningful or "stop" words, as they are usually known.

Thesauri

Computerised analysis and indexing of references and abstracts is obviously a very effective technique, but on its own it cannot satisfy every

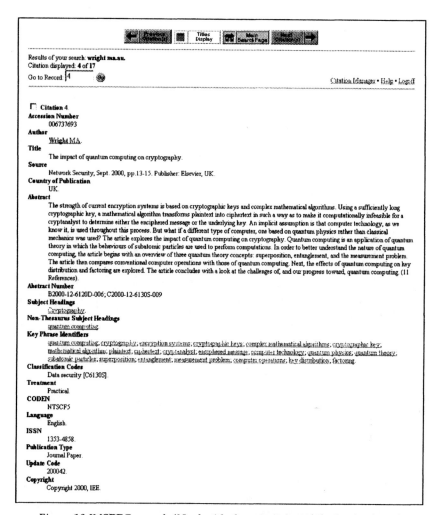

Figure 18 INSPEC record. (Used with the permission of the Institution of Electrical Engineers, EDINA and OVID Technologies Inc.)

need. One of the problems searchers face when using databases such as *MEDLINE* or *INSPEC* is that they may unwittingly be using different keywords to describe the subject than those used by the authors of the article. To give an example, the common painkiller *aspirin* may be referred to as *ethylsalicylate*, its scientific name. The word *painkiller* too is less likely to be used than the term *analgesic* by researchers.

The way many database producers get round this difficulty is by providing a thesaurus of subject terms used to index the records. A thesaurus, sometimes referred to as a "controlled vocabulary", is basically a collection of carefully chosen keywords used to describe a subject field. As part of the production of the database, professional indexing staff will scan the content of articles to be included, allocating appropriate keywords, often called "descriptors" or "controlled terms", from the thesaurus to the articles concerned. These keywords are then built up into another subject index of descriptor keywords.

For instance the database producers of *MEDLINE* use a thesaurus named *Medical Subject Headings* or *MeSH*. In *MeSH* the descriptor *Herpes labialis* is used as the chosen keyword for *cold sores*. If, as with *Herpes labialis*, a subject or compound can be described by any one of several keywords or synonyms, a thesaurus will indicate which is the preferred choice, and link the keywords not selected to the one which has been, as shown in Figure 19. To avoid confusion over the meaning of a descriptor, some explanatory text, usually known as a "scope note", is included.

A thesaurus should also show the position of the chosen keyword in the hierarchy or tree structure of descriptors. With *Herpes labialis*, it can be seen that the term first appears towards the bottom of the *Diseases* category, after *Herpes simplex*. In fact *Herpes labialis*, like many other descriptors, appears in more than one place in the *MeSH* hierarchy. This is because *Herpes labialis* can be approached from several aspects – for example, as a viral skin disease, as a lip disease and as an infectious skin disease. These other subcategories could be useful as a prompt to remind a searcher that there are related topics, where there might also be relevant information.

At first sight, the effort and cost involved for database producers in constructing a thesaurus and ensuring that all new articles are scanned by professional indexing staff might seem excessive, given that subject indexes can be generated automatically by computerised techniques. For someone needing a few articles as background reading, a quick search based on keywords taken from the title and abstract of a paper is often likely to be sufficient. The benefits of the thesaurus approach become more apparent however, if you need to pinpoint specific information or are finding hundreds of articles retrieved by each keyword.

Classification codes

Some database producers also include other features in their records to provide for alternative ways of searching. One technique used by some bibliographic databases is to give each paper a classification code, as an additional way of "describing" its content. The *INSPEC* record in Figure 18, for instance, has been allocated the code for data security [C6130S]. Patent applications are routinely allocated classification codes. More than one type of code is often allocated to patents. British patents are given a domestic code, and an International Classification one, as shown in Figure 2 on page 8. The facility to use classification codes for searching can be very useful, particularly if a topic is hard to describe using

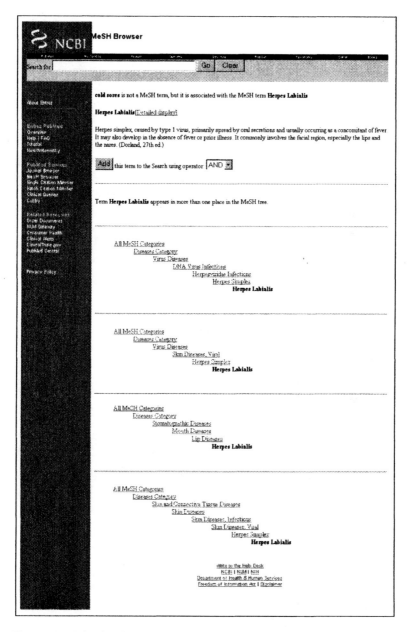

Figure 19: Medical Subject Headings (MeSH) browser (PubMed is a registered trademark of the US National Library of Medicine.)

keywords – the titles of patents, for instance, can be phrased to obscure rather than clarify their scope.

Registry Numbers

Another technique is the Registry Number system, pioneered and owned by *Chemical Abstracts,* one of the world's premier bibliographic databases. In addition to abstracts of the huge number of articles and patents published in chemistry, the database also has records of over 30 million chemical substances.

Chemical Abstracts gives each substance an identifier, known as a CAS Registry Number®. The CAS Registry Number – or its abbreviation RN – does not itself have any in-built chemical significance. Its value lies in the fact that it is a unique identifier, linking all the names, whether these are trivial, proprietary, non-systematic or generic, to the correct molecular structure. Figure 20 shows how the drug paracetamol is linked to its chemical name, N-(4-hydroxyphenyl)-acetamide, with the Registry Number [103-90-2] in *The Index Guide,* the list used by *Chemical Abstracts.* These Registry Numbers are obviously of value when searching *Chemical Abstracts,* but they are also used widely by other bibliographic databases including *MEDLINE* and *INSPEC* databases.

Paraceisin D
See ***Saturnisporin SA III [95298–69–2]***
Paracentrone
See ***3,5,7,9,11,13,15,17–Octadecaoctaen–2–one, 18–(2,4–dihydroxy–2,6,6–trimethylcyclohexylidene)–3,7,12,16–tetramethyl–, [2R–[1R*,(3E,5E,7E,9E,11E,13E,15E),2α,4β]]–[31190–20–2]***
Paracetamol
See ***Acetamide, N–(4–hydroxyphenyl)– [103–90–2]***
Parachlor
See ***Phosphorothioic acid, esters, O,O–dimethyl O–(4–nitrophenyl) ester, mixt. with 1,1'–(2,2,2–trichloroethylidene)bis[4–chlorobenzene] [8064–95–7]***
Parachlor 250
See ***Paraffin oils,*** **chloro**
Parachlor 380
See ***Paraffin waxes,*** **chloro**
Parachloral
See ***1,3,5–Trioxane, 2,4,6–tris(trichloromethyl)–[3562–18–3]***
α–Parachloral
See ***1,3,5–Trioxane, 2,4,6–tris(trichloromethyl)–, (2α,4α,6β)– [75597–94–3]***
β–Parachloral
See ***1,3,5–Trioxane, 2,4,6–tris(trichloromethyl)–, (2α,4α,6α)– [75597–95–4]***
Parachlor Red
See ***2–Naphthalenol, 1–[(4–chloro–2–nitrophenyl)azo]– [6410–13–5]***

Figure 20: Chemical Abstracts index guide. (CAS information is reprinted by permission of the American Chemical Society.)

Planning a search

Traditionally librarians have always laid emphasis on planning an information search, though it has to be said that in practice most users throw themselves straight into the process. Understandable as this is, it is a pity in many ways – most people only have limited time available for searching so it is important to use it as effectively as possible.

There are basically three stages involved in planning a search:

- defining the search topic and breaking it down into its component parts
- deciding which keywords should be used
- choosing a databases or databases to search.

Defining the search topic

Many search topics could be described as "woolly" initially, and benefit from clarifying the emphasis and limits. Take for example a search for information on the effects of a vegetarian diet on health. Is the search to cover all aspects of health or concentrate on particular organs or functions such as the heart and blood pressure? How is a vegetarian diet to be defined? Are the limits to be tightly drawn to exclude people who eat fish, but not meat? What about people who also eat no dairy products? Asking these sort of questions helps to break a topic down into its component parts, a useful preparation when searching bibliographic databases.

These databases make use of a type of set theory called Boolean logic, although this is not always apparent to the user. With Boolean logic, a topic is broken down into its separate parts, known as concepts. For example, a search for information on the reliability of biometric techniques – authenticating the identity an individual using physiological characteristics such as palm prints, retina scans or iris patterns – could be considered as two main concepts: *biometrics* and *reliability*. A search for information on the risks involved in the treatment of the behavioural problem, attention-deficit hyperactivity disorder (ADHD), with the drug Ritalin can be broken down into three main concepts: *attention-deficit hyperactivity disorder*, *Ritalin* and *risk*. A few, though not many, searches consist only of one concept – everything on *stem cells*, for example.

The information-retrieval software used to carry out searches operates by finding all the references in the database about each concept, and then combining them in such a way that the output only consists of those references which include all the concepts. The three Boolean logic operators or links – "AND", "OR" and "NOT" – are used to join the different concepts together. The combination of concepts using these Boolean operators is usually illustrated by means of Venn diagrams, as in Figure 21.

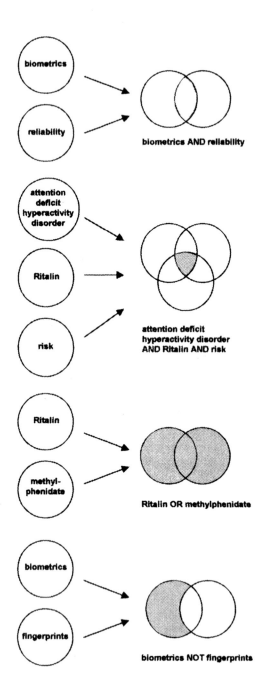

Figure 21: Examples of Boolean logic

Using "AND" logic narrows down a search. If the concepts *biometrics* and *reliability* are combined using "AND", the shaded section where the two circles intersect will represent the references containing both concepts, that is, *biometrics* AND *reliability*. It can be seen that combining the three concepts *attention-deficit hyperactivity disorder* AND *Ritalin* AND *risk* produces an even smaller common set. Using "OR" logic widens a search. In the latter search, *Ritalin* could be referred to by its chemical name, *methylphenidate*. References containing either *Ritalin* OR *methylphenidate* can be combined to create a larger group or set.

"NOT" logic is used to exclude a particular concept. A search for information on biometric techniques but specifically excluding fingerprints would consist of two concepts, *biometrics* and *fingerprints*. As Figure 21 shows, when these two concepts are combined using "NOT" logic, a smaller set is produced. "NOT" logic needs to be used with care because there is a danger of missing relevant references. As well as excluding those papers specifically about fingerprinting, any references dealing with biometric techniques in general, but which also mention fingerprinting, would also be lost.

Choosing keywords

Once a search topic has been broken down into its concepts, the keywords or subject terms need to be considered. Sometimes only one term is necessary – *attention-deficit hyperactivity disorder*, for example, has a clearly defined meaning with no obvious synonyms, apart from its acronym, *ADHD*.

Frequently, however, a concept may require several keywords to define it adequately. For example, in addition to *reliability* the term *robust* is often used to define a system that must stand up to rigorous use. Because the search software makes a character-by-character comparison of the keywords input with the index terms in the database, it is usually also necessary to indicate alternative spellings. Probably the easiest to remember are the obvious differences such as the American spelling of *sulfur*, as opposed to the British version, *sulphur*. Sometimes the harder ones to avoid are the less obvious differences such as the American spellings of *color, behavior* and *aluminum*. Word endings also need to be borne in mind, to find both the singular or plural version of keywords, and adjectives and nouns such as *bacterial* or *bacteria*.

If you have some familiarity with a topic, you will probably be aware of some variant spellings and word endings. Although you may have to hunt around an interface to find them, help is available on many systems via the index files. These are the lists of all the searchable words in the database, and can be used as a checklist. An example from the large psychology database *PsycINFO*, available on the *OCLC FirstSearch* system, is shown in Figure 22. In addition, many databases have online vocabularies or a thesaurus such as *Medical Subject Headings (MeSH)*, linking a keyword input by a user to the subject headings used in the database to describe the topic.

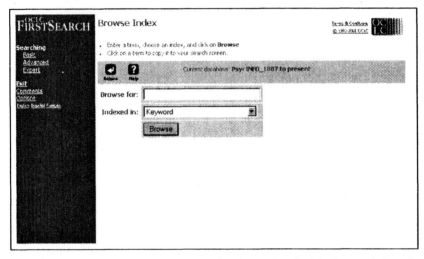

Figure 22: OCLC FirstSearch browse index. (Reproduced with the permission of OCLC Online Computer Library Center, Inc.)

Choosing a bibliographic database

An important aspect of any information search is the choice of a suitable bibliographic database or databases. If you are new to a subject field, how do you choose the best one for your topic? Although there are some very useful bibliographic databases which are free to use, many are subscription based. Organisations sign licences and pay annual fees to give their users the right to search these databases. To some extent therefore the decision is taken out of your hands, because you are likely mainly to be choosing from the databases provided by your library or information service. These databases will have been selected to reflect the subject interests of the organisation the LIS serves. If a subject field has been of interest for some time it is probable that a subscription to a relevant bibliographic database will already exist.

The large number of bibliographic databases produced make it impossible to give a complete inventory, but a list of the some of most widely available and heavily used ones is given in Table 1. A list of versions of databases free to use (at the time of writing) is given in Table 2.

Database	Producer	Subject field
BIOSIS Previews	BIOSIS Inc	Biological and biomedical sciences
CAB Abstracts	CAB International	Agriculture, forestry, human health and nutrition, animal health and conservation
Chemical Abstracts	American Chemical Society	Chemistry
Ei Compendex	Engineering Information	All subject fields in engineering
EMBASE	Elsevier Science	Human medicine, biomedicine and pharmacology
INSPEC	Institution of Engineers	Computer science, electrical and electronic engineering and physics
Medline	US National Library of Medicine	Human medicine and related biomedical research
PsycINFO	American Psychological Association	Psychology and behavioural topics from related disciplines
Science Citation Index (Web of Science)	ISI	All subject fields in science and technology

Table 1 Some bibliographic databases

It may well be that you will be faced with a choice between two or three databases, particularly if you are working in a subject field on the fringe of several disciplines. Toxicology, for instance, is generally considered to be a branch of medical science, but the study of the toxic effects of chemicals on plants and animals is also of interest to biologists and chemists. Because of this, toxicological literature is covered by three large bibliographic databases – *Chemical Abstracts,* covering all branches of chemistry, *BIOSIS,* covering biological sciences, and *MEDLINE,* mentioned earlier in this chapter.

If you find yourself in this situation, there are two factors which are worth bearing in mind when deciding which database to use:

- The type of subject information which has been included. Although a subject field may be covered by several databases, the emphasis in each will tend to be different. To go back to our example of toxicology, it would be reasonable to expect that *MEDLINE* would concentrate on covering toxicological information from the medical angle, and that *BIOSIS* would emphasise the effect of toxins on the environment.

- The type of information included. Some databases restrict themselves solely to covering articles published in journals, while others also include conference papers. Even large databases can be very selective when it comes to including reports, books and theses, and with the exception of *Chemical Abstracts* most exclude patents completely. If you are specifically looking for the type of information found in patents, you are probably best advised to use the specialised patent databases. If you suspect that quite a lot of work in the subject field is written up in report form rather than as papers in journals, then it may also be worth searching a database specifically covering these. A good starting point would be the *NTIS Electronic Catalog,* listed in Table 2.

Bearing these two factors in mind, how can you find out without wasting much time what a database covers? The first thing is to look for a guide, or leaflet about the database. Most libraries and information units either produce their own short guides or buy in documentation from database producers, which you should be able to take away to study. Secondly most databases also publish a list, such as the one produced by *INSPEC* shown in Figure 23, of the journals which are scanned for articles. If you know of, or regularly browse through, several journals in a subject field, it is also worth checking to see if these are covered by the database. Sometimes these lists will be available in printed form, but it is more likely that you will have to log onto the database in question to see what is covered.

Database	Description	Provider	Web address
Agricola	Articles, books, reports, etc. in agriculture and related disciplines.	US National Agricultural Library	http://www.nalusda.gov/ag98/
CANCERLIT	Articles, conference proceedings, books, reports and theses.	US National Cancer Institute	http://cnetdb.nci.nih.gov/
Digital Dissertations	Two most recent years of theses from North American and European universities.	UMI ProQuest	http://wwwlib.umi.com/dissertations/
DOE Reports	Scientific and technical reports sponsored by the DOE.	US Department of Energy, Office of Scientific and Technical Information	http://www.osti.gov/index.html
Esp@cenet	30 million patent applications published worldwide, including UK	European Patent Office	http://gb.espacenet.com
GrayLIT Network	US government full-text technical reports	US Department of Energy, Office of Scientific and Technical Information	http://www.osti.gov/graylit/
NASA Astrophysics Data System	Articles and pre-prints in astronomical, planetary sciences, solar physics plus extensive coverage of physics and instrumentation	NASA	http://ukads.nottingham.ac.uk

Table 2 Some freely accessible bibliographic databases

Database	Description	Provider	Web address
NTIS Electronic Catalog	Reports of US government-sponsored scientific and technical research.	National Technical Information Service, US Dept. of Commerce	http://www.ntis.gov/search.htm
Offshore Engineering Information Service	Oil and gas exploration and production.	Heriot-Watt University, Edinburgh	http://www.eevl.ac.uk/offshore/
PubMed	MEDLINE plus additional life sciences journals.	US National Library of Medicine	http://www.ncbi.nlm.nih.gov/PubMed
RAM Recent Advances in Manufacturing	Articles, books, videos and conference proceedings in manufacturing and related areas	Nottingham Trent University and the Edinburgh Engineering Virtual Library (EEVL)	http://www.eevl.ac.uk/ram/
TOXNET	Group of databases covering toxicology, hazardous chemicals and related areas.	US National Library of Medicine	http://toxnet.nlm.nih.gov/
TRIS	Transportation Research Information Services Database	National Academy of Sciences, Transportation Research Board	http://199.79.179.82/sundev/search.cfm
USPTO	US patents dating back to 1970	US Patent and Trademark Office	http://www.uspto.gov/main/patents.htm

Term	Postings
O V I D	Index Display ? Help

Perform Search ◀ Back of Index   🏠 Main Search Page   Forward in Index ▶

Enter a new start term: [   ] Go

Choose from among the following index entries:

Term	Postings
☐ electromotion.jn.	133
☐ electromyography & clinical neurophysiology.jn.	259
☐ electron technology warsaw.jn.	387
☐ electronic business.jn.	2
☐ electronic business law reports.jn.	5
☐ electronic business today.jn.	8
☐ electronic commerce research.jn.	19
☐ electronic commerce world.jn.	218
☐ electronic components & materials.jn.	69
☐ electronic design.jn.	793
☐ electronic engineering.jn.	429
☐ electronic journal of information technology in construction.jn.	16
☐ electronic journal on information systems in developing countries.jn.	5
☐ electronic learning.jn.	1
☐ electronic library.jn.	203
☐ electronic markets.jn.	88
☐ electronic modeling.pj.	134
☐ electronic notes in theoretical computer science.jn.	410
☐ electronic packaging & production.jn.	306
☐ electronic product design.jn.	470
☐ electronic production london.jn.	5
☐ electronic publishing origination dissemination & design.jn.	24
☐ electronic technology london.jn.	1
☐ electronic transactions on numerical analysis.jn.	15
☐ electronica y fisica aplicada.jn.	1
☐ electronics & communication engineering journal.jn.	153
☐ electronics & communications in japan part 1 communications english translation of denshi tsushin gakkai ronbunshi.jn	693
☐ electronics & communications in japan part 2 electronics english translation of denshi tsushin gakkai ronbunshi.jn.	608
☐ electronics & communications in japan part iii fundamental electronic science.jn.	741
☐ electronics industry new malden england.jn.	2

Perform Search ◀ Back of Index   🏠 Main Search Page   Forward in Index ▶

Copyright (c) 1999-2001 Ovid Technologies, Inc.
Version: rel4.1.1, SourceID: 1.4582.1.605

Figure 23: Journals index display. (Used with the permission of the Institution of Electrical Engineers, EDINA and OVID Technologies Inc.)

Access

Database producers or suppliers basically have two options open to them in marketing their information. One is for the producer itself to market the database, either on CD-ROM, or via the Internet on its own Web site. If the database is sold on CD-ROM then the producer will also need to supply information-retrieval software for searching the information on the disc or discs. If the producer provides access to the database on its own Web site, it will also need to supply a computer system for storing the information, and the information-retrieval software for searching. Unless the database is free to use, the producer also needs to put in place a mechanism to restrict access to its paying customers.

The second option is to make an arrangement with another organisation, which takes on the function of a service provider, supplying the computer system, the information-retrieval software and the general tasks of controlling access to the information. There are a large number of organisations which act as service providers in this way including universities and non-profit-making organisations, as well as companies. Bibliographic databases which are in demand by users may be obtained from several different service providers. *MEDLINE,* for example, is available free directly from the National Library of Medicine itself as the service *"PubMed"*, and from several other organisations, including those listed in Table 2. It can also be purchased by libraries and information units on CD-ROM and via the Web from several different service providers.

This situation can be confusing to users, but it may help to remember that the different versions are all based on the same original bibliographic data. The subject coverage and the journals indexed are the same. What does vary is the way each service provider processes the data, and the interface they provide to search for the information contained. One service provider, for example, may decide to divide a database into several different time periods, such as 1990–1994, 1994–1998, 1999–. Another service provider of the same database may opt to provide one large file covering the span from 1990 to date. Libraries and information units use a range of criteria when choosing the versions of bibliographic databases to which they subscribe. Factors which affect the decision include how easy an interface is to use, the searching facilities available (some versions of a database provide more advanced features than others), the average response time, and of course the cost.

Data centres

In the UK the higher education community has taken a very active role in this area, establishing a number of service providers known as data centres – *BIDS, NISS, MIMAS* and *EDINA*. The first to be set up, and possibly still most well known, is *BIDS* (the acronym initially stood for Bath Information Data Service), based at the University of Bath. *NISS* (National

Information Services and Systems) is also based at Bath University. *MIMAS* (Manchester Information and Associated Services) and *EDINA* (Edinburgh Data and Information Access) are based at the universities of Manchester and Edinburgh respectively. Collectively these four centres co-ordinate access to most of the major bibliographic databases likely to be needed by British university students, staff and researchers in science, engineering and medicine. The system is designed to be "free at the point of use". University libraries pay for subscriptions to relevant databases, with their students and staff then being able to carry out as many searches as they wish.

CD-ROM

As mentioned earlier, databases marketed on CD-ROMs also need to be supplied with their own information-retrieval software, which is used to search the information. When the databases are bought by libraries and information units, these can either be set up as "stand-alone" or "networked" systems. In a stand-alone system, the disc is searched directly from the CD-ROM drive on a PC, just as happens when a CD-ROM is used on a PC at home. There are two disadvantages though to this arrangement – only one person at a time can search a database, and use is restricted to one physical location in the library or information unit. "Desk-top access" – enabling a user to search from a laboratory, office, or another work location – is not possible. To get round this problem, where operationally feasible, libraries and information units network their CD-ROM databases, loading the information onto a server (a computer system). With this type of networked system, users can search a CD-ROM database from workstations outside the library building itself.

Usernames and passwords

Since most bibliographic databases are not free services, an authentication or security check is necessarily involved when logging on. The way this is achieved varies to some extent, depending on the local computer set-up and on the supplier or service provider hosting the database, but if you are based in a university or college, connecting to a Web-based database may involve two authentication steps:

- entering a username and password, identifying yourself to the local computer network
- entering a separate, additional username and password, identifying your organisation and yourself as a *bona fide* user to the supplier or service provider whose database you want to search.

If you are using a CD-ROM database on a computer or network server at your organisation, then this second step will probably not be necessary.

One of the major irritations faced by searchers is the need to have separate usernames and passwords for different services. Unless the information is vital, there is a temptation to give up at this point, if a username and password are not immediately to hand. In an effort to improve this situation, a generic username and password system called ATHENS (Access To Higher Education via NISS Authentication System) has been developed, and is now in widespread use in universities and colleges in the UK.

ATHENS usernames and passwords fall in to two categories:

- "Access Accounts" in which a username and password can be used by a number of separate people, but only from known locations such as a university campus or research institute

- "Personal Accounts", in which a username and password can be used only by an individual, but from any location, including home. A Personal Account username will look something like "astlambertr", where the first three letters represent an abbreviation of the name of the organisation, followed by the name of the individual concerned.

In the course of searching, you are likely to encounter another authentication technique, based on the fact that each computer on the Internet has a unique identifying number, known as its IP (Internet Protocol) address. With this technique the library or information unit gives the supplier or service provider a list of the IP addresses of all the computers in the organisation, which are entitled to have access to the databases concerned. It is a popular approach because it avoids having to type in any username and password. If you want to search one of these databases from your home or other non-work location, ask your library or information centre if it can give you with an appropriate username and password, as your workstation will not be "recognised" by the supplier or service provider's computer system.

Search software

Most people are likely to use more than one bibliographic database in the course of their work, which means getting used to the layout of different interfaces, and the specific search facilities available. Although proprietary interfaces vary, there are common functions which underpin the process of searching. If you know what these are, then you can look for the way a function has been implemented in the interface you are using. The main ones of which to be aware are listed below.

- The use of the Boolean operators and the order in which these are applied. A simple search, for example, on the cloning of sheep could be entered as *sheep* AND *cloning*, using the Boolean operator AND to combine the two keywords. With more complex searches the order of the Boolean operators needs to be considered. A search for authentication systems using retina scans or iris patterns would be best entered as (*retina* OR *iris*) AND *authentication*. Enclosing *iris* and *retina* in parentheses instructs the computer system to process this expression of keywords first. If the keywords were entered as *retina* OR *iris* AND *authentication*, the system would retrieve any records including *retina*, then all records including *iris,* but then only search for *authentication* in the latter set. The actual order in which the Boolean operators are executed can vary to some extent, depending on the search software used. Information on this should be available from the Help screens on the interface, but generally speaking enclosing expressions in parentheses will ensure that these are executed first.

- Free text or uncontrolled searching – this is the most common way of finding information. It involves the keywords input being matched with the indexes containing all the significant words in the titles of articles, abstracts and subject index terms. Any item containing the keywords – wherever these appear in the record – will be retrieved. The record in Figure 17 for example, would have been found by typing in the keywords *green tea* as these appear in the abstract. It can be a good way of getting an overview of what is in a database, but is not the most precise method of searching.

- Controlled searching – this way of searching utilises the subject index terms. The keywords input are only matched against with the subject index terms added by the professional indexers. The record in Figure 17 would not have been retrieved using *green tea* as this is not a subject heading in *MEDLINE*. Controlled searching is a more precise way of finding information because it makes use of the work by the professional indexing staff of the database. As they scan the content of articles to be included in the database, they determine which keywords should be used to describe the scope and emphasis of the content.

- Proximity searching – this is a means of looking for two or more keywords adjacent or in very close position to each other. It is similar in principle to the process used by search engines of enclosing keywords in quotation marks, outlined in Chapter 2. Some interfaces follow the same practice of using quotation marks, but many others use different techniques. This could be a pull-down menu where you are given the choice of whether you want the keywords adjacent to each other or within a specified number of other words, e.g. within 10 or 20 words. Many interfaces provide what are known as "adjacency operators", where you can type in an instruction such as *skin ADJ cancer*, to show that you want the two keywords next to each other. It is worth checking to see what proximity operators are used, as if you just leave a space between two words such as *skin cancer*, it will depend on the interface how this is interpreted. Some interfaces might automatically search for the keywords as a phrase, but some might interpret the space as an implicit Boolean "AND". The system would then retrieve any references containing these two keywords *skin* AND *cancer* wherever the location in the record. Other interfaces might interpret it as *skin* OR *cancer*, so that you could get records about other skin diseases or other types of cancer.

- Truncation – this is simply a way of retrieving all the variant spellings or word endings of the keywords. Many interfaces use an asterisk (*) as truncation symbol, so if you wanted all the variants of the keyword *prediction*, you could enter it as *predict** to get *predictable*, *prediction*, *predictions* or *predicting*. Others use a dollar sign ($) or a question mark (?). The truncation symbol can often also be used as a wildcard, to search for variant spellings such as sul*ur, to find sulphur or sulfur. Each system will have specific rules on how the symbols can be used, which will be detailed in the Help screens.

- Limiting – this is a way of decreasing the number of references obtained, while at the same time increasing the relevancy. Systems vary in what is available, but common restrictions include limiting a search so that only records where the keyword appears in the title of the article are retrieved, or limiting the results to English-language items only. Another useful limit that is often available is to restrict the output to review articles. The limits available depend both on the way the service provider has processed the database and on the nature of the information. With *MEDLINE*, for instance, depending on the version searched, it is possible to limit references found to studies by gender or to specific age groups.

- Search history – this is a way of displaying on screen all the previous combinations of keywords entered during the search. With some systems only the most recent keywords entered will be displayed, but using the search history function will enable you to review all the previous ones. A history function comes in to its own in a long search, when it is easy to become confused as to which combinations of keywords have been tried before.

- Re-using sets or groups of references – systems usually allocate a set number to each group of records retrieved. If you want to combine that set with a new keyword, then the set number can often be used, rather than typing in all the keywords again. A symbol may be used to represent the set, e.g. #3 AND *authentication*. If so it is necessary to use this as otherwise the system would be searching for the number "3" in all records in the database.

- Order of display – probably the commonest approach is for the records retrieved in a search to be shown in reverse order of the date they were added to the database. Some systems also provide the option of relevance ranking, with the records considered to be the closest match to the query being displayed first. The criteria used for relevance ranking may include calculations of the number of times a keyword appears in the record, an estimate of the uniqueness of a keyword, and the degree of proximity of keywords, with those closer together being allocated a higher relevance.

- Output – the options are usually either saving to disk, emailing, printing, or copying and pasting into a word-processing package.

- Saved searches – this function, offered by many service providers, enables the search strategy (the combination of keywords used) to be stored after logging off. The search strategy is then available next time you log onto the database, without having to type in all the keywords again. This can be useful if you get interrupted during a search, and need to resume later in the day. It also has benefits as a current-awareness tool, because the search strategy can be matched regularly with new records added to the database, as outlined further in Chapter 6.

As may be apparent, the way these functions are implemented in practice is dependent on the proprietary software in use. For example with some systems you would need to input the Boolean operators, typing in the keywords *sheep* "AND" *cloning*. In other systems you might need to type the keywords into a form, so that *sheep* is entered on the first line of the form, *cloning* on the second, with a pull-down menu being provided listing the three Boolean operators, from which you would choose AND. Interfaces are designed to be intuitive to users, so to a large extent the screen display should prompt and guide you towards the function you need, but it will not be perfect. The Help facility should be used to check for the specifics such as which adjacency operators can be used, or where it is not clear if a function is available, or how it is implemented. Do try to make of use the Help screens – it may take a few minutes more, but it will save time in the long run.

Search examples

The three searches in Figures 24, 25 and 26 have been chosen to show a range of the functions outlined above. The first two are subject searches, using the *MEDLINE* and *INSPEC* bibliographic databases. The third is a "citation search", starting with a landmark article published in 1997, the aim being to find out which more recent articles have made reference to the original research work.

The effectiveness of Ritalin on the treatment of ADHD (attention-deficit hyperactivity disorder)
This short search was carried out using the *PubMed* version of the *MEDLINE* database. As listed in Table 2, *PubMed* is freely available for anyone to search on the Web at *http://www.ncbi.nlm.nih.gov/PubMed/*

The search began by typing in *ADHD*, combining this with either *Ritalin* or its chemical name *methylphenidate* (Figures 24a and 24b), the search finding 343 items. Although some of these looked as if they dealt with the effectiveness of Ritalin, others did not seem that relevant. Three hundred references is a large number to scan, too, so it seemed appropriate to narrow the search down.

The next step was to use the small History "button" underneath the search box to check the symbol and set or group number for the references already retrieved. As Figure 24c shows, the # symbol is used by *PubMed* to represent a previous set. The search was then refined by entering #1 AND *effectiveness*, resulting in 19 items, as shown in Figure 24d.

The reliability of voiceprints – a technique making use of a speaker's voice as a means of authentication
This search was carried out using the *INSPEC* database, published by the Institution of Electrical Engineers. *INSPEC*, listed in Table 1, covers computer science, electrical and electronic engineering and physics. The

Figure 24a: Screen display from PubMed. *(PubMed is a registered trademark of the US National Library of Medicine.)*

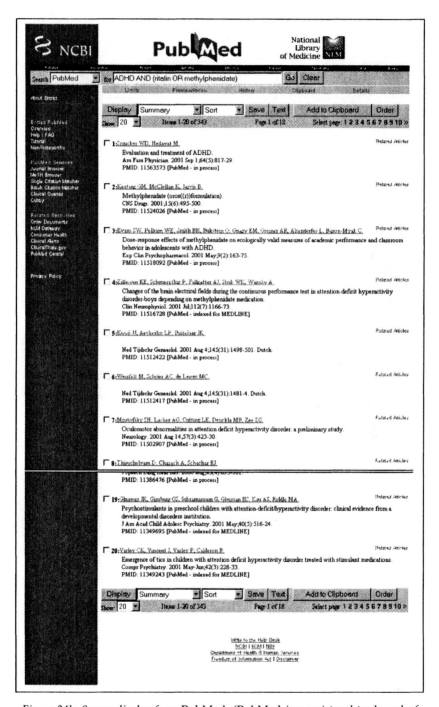

Figure 24b: Screen display from PubMed. (PubMed *is a registered trademark of the US National Library of Medicine.)*

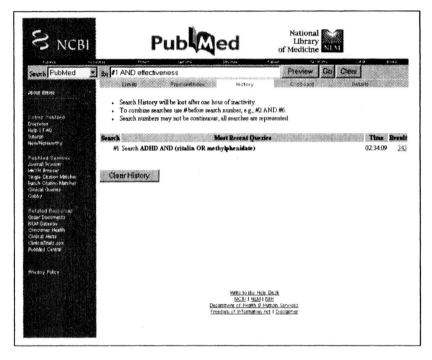

Figure 24c: Screen display from PubMed. *(PubMed is a registered trademark of the US National Library of Medicine.)*

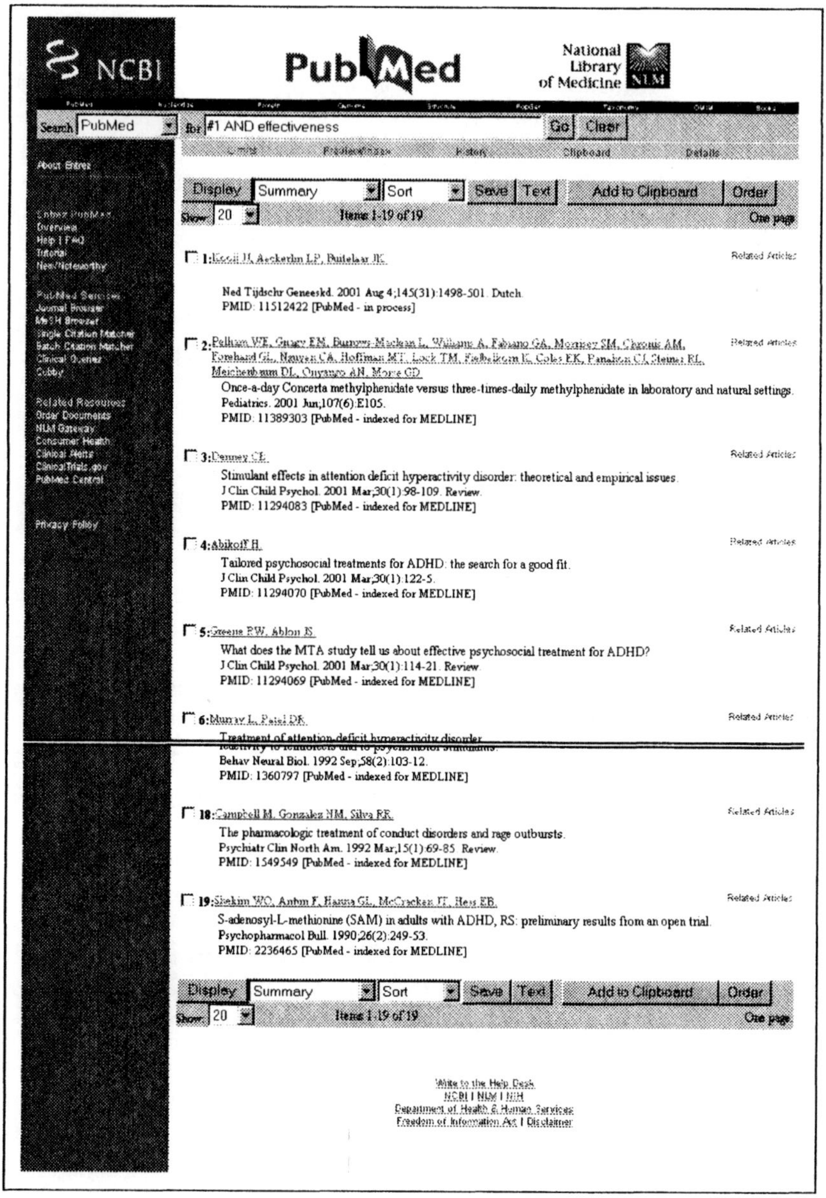

Figure 24d: Screen display from PubMed. (PubMed *is a registered trademark of the US National Library of Medicine.*)

example below was carried out using the *INSPEC* database hosted at the EDINA data centre. This particular version of *INSPEC* on *EDINA*, which uses OVID search software, is only available to universities and other higher education institutions in the UK, who have paid for subscriptions. Like many other bibliographic databases, *INSPEC* is available worldwide both via the Web and on CD-ROM from a range of service providers and suppliers. If you think *INSPEC* would be useful to you, ask your library or information centre if it subscribes to the database.

The database is divided into several time periods – this search was limited to the time period 1996 onwards, though it is possible to search back as far as 1969 on *EDINA*. The OVID software, which is widely used for searching bibliographic databases, has two different interfaces – Basic and Advanced. The Advanced interface was used, as this provided more search options.

The system was instructed to retrieve any items containing *reliab$*, using the truncation symbol $ to find records containing either keywords *reliable* and *reliability* (Figure 25a). Nearly 62,000 items were found, the first few of which are shown in Figure 25b. The next step was to type in *voiceprint$* to find records mentioning voiceprint or prints (Figure 25c). As Figure 25d shows only seven items were found – this is a low output and it would be reasonable to expect that more work had been published on this topic.

One feature of the OVID search software is that keywords can be linked to the online thesaurus by putting a tick in the "Map term to Subject Heading" box, as shown in Figure 25e. The search was repeated using this feature, giving a "Mapping Display" of possible Subject Headings (Figure 25f). Speaker recognition was selected using the tick box and the Continue button activated. As this produced over 700 items (Figure 25g), the search was narrowed down by combining this set with the earlier set on reliability, using the Combine Searches function (Figure 25h). Combining the two sets produced 30 references (Figure 25i).

Tracing a paper "forward in time"
Either as a result of information passed on to them by colleagues, or from their own searches, most people are likely to find at least one article of particular importance to their project. Other researchers are also likely to have drawn upon the work in this paper and will conse-

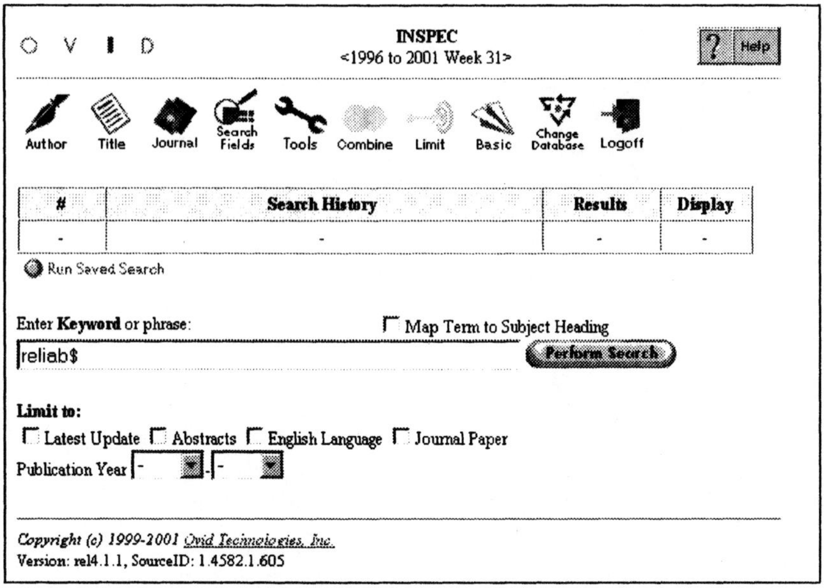

Figure 25a: INSPEC *on* EDINA *using OVID search software. (Used with the permission of the Institution of Electrical Engineers, EDINA and OVID Technologies Inc.)*

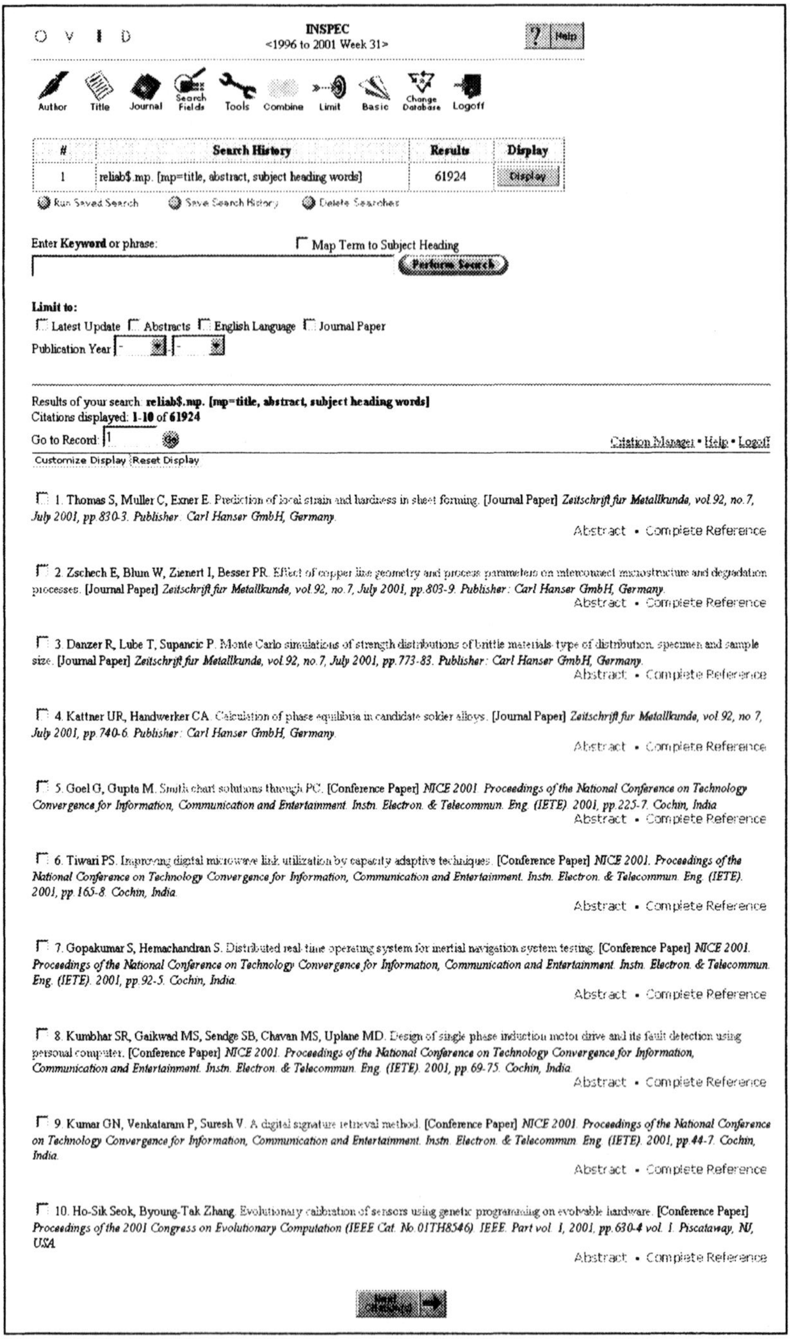

Figure 25b: INSPEC *on EDINA using OVID search software. (Used with the permission of the Institution of Electrical Engineers, EDINA and OVID Technologies Inc.)*

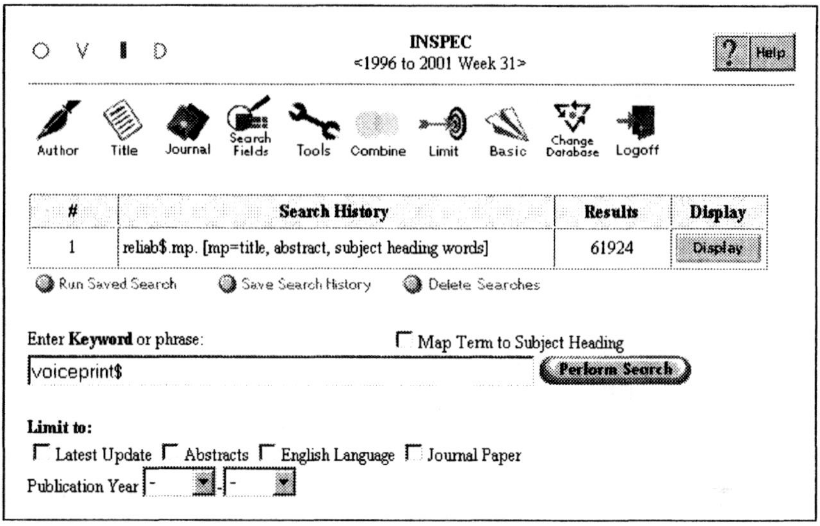

Figure 25c: INSPEC *on* EDINA *using OVID search software. (Used with the permission of the Institution of Electrical Engineers, EDINA and OVID Technologies Inc.)*

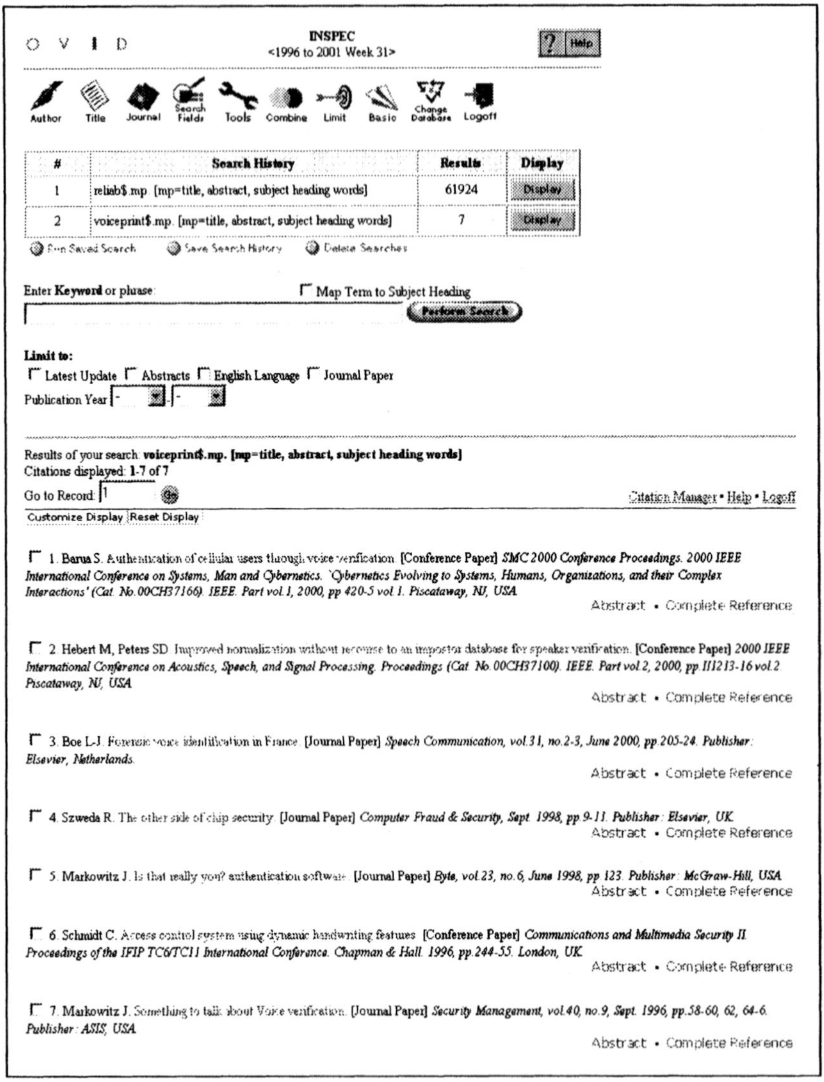

Figure 25d: INSPEC *on EDINA using OVID search software. (Used with the permission of the Institution of Electrical Engineers, EDINA and OVID Technologies Inc.)*

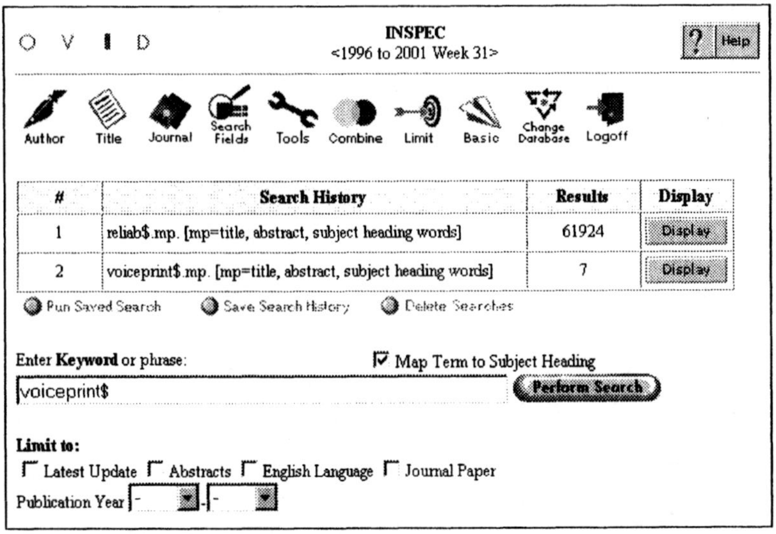

Figure 25e: INSPEC *on* EDINA *using OVID search software. (Used with the permission of the Institution of Electrical Engineers, EDINA and OVID Technologies Inc.)*

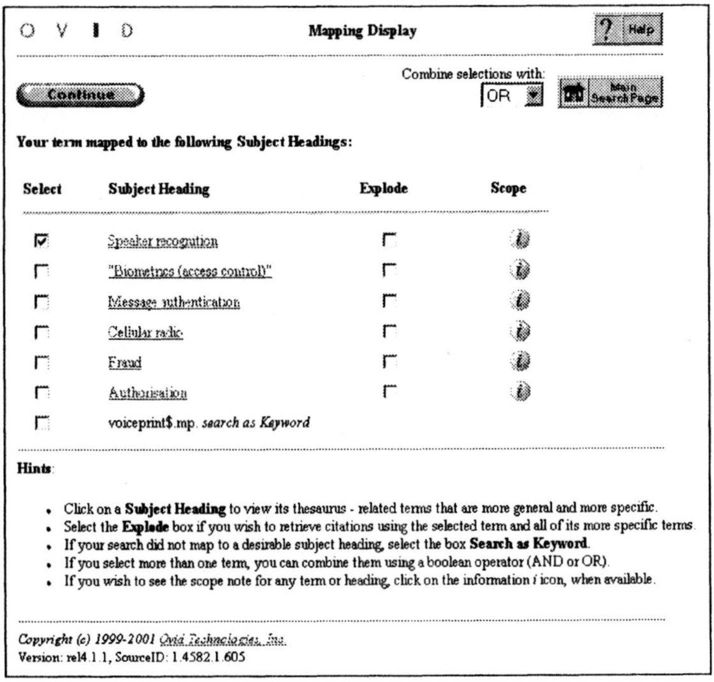

Figure 25f: INSPEC *on* EDINA *using OVID search software. (Used with the permission of the Institution of Electrical Engineers, EDINA and OVID Technologies Inc.)*

O V I D   **INSPEC**   ? Help
<1996 to 2001 Week 31>

Author   Title   Journal   Search Fields   Tools   Combine   Limit   Basic   Change Database   Logoff

#	Search History	Results	Display
1	reliab$.mp. [mp=title, abstract, subject heading words]	61924	Display
2	voiceprint$.mp. [mp=title, abstract, subject heading words]	7	Display
3	Speaker recognition/	733	Display

Run Saved Search   Save Search history   Delete Searches

Enter **Keyword** or phrase   ☑ Map Term to Subject Heading

Perform Search

Limit to:
☐ Latest Update ☐ Abstracts ☐ English Language ☐ Journal Paper
Publication Year [ ] - [ ]

Results of your search: **Speaker recognition/**
Citations displayed: 1-10 of 733
Go to Record: 1   Citation Manager • Help • Logoff
Customize Display Reset Display

☐ 1. Vanathi PT, Pushparaj K, Shanmugham A, Balaji V, Kumar TS. Implementation of speaker verification system using simple BP, recurrent neural networks and dynamic time warping techniques. [Conference Paper] *NICE 2001. Proceedings of the National Conference on Technology Convergence for Information, Communication and Entertainment. Instn. Electron. & Telecommun. Eng. (IETE).* 2001, pp.16-20. Cochin, India.
Abstract • Complete Reference

☐ 2. Hao Pan, Zhu-Pei Liang, Huang TS. Fusing audio and visual features of speech. [Conference Paper] *Proceedings 2000 International Conference on Image Processing (Cat. No.00CH37101). IEEE. Part vol 3,* 2000, pp.214-17 vol 3. Piscataway, NJ, USA.
Abstract • Complete Reference

☐ 3. Miyajima C, Hattori Y, Tokuda K, Masuko T, Kobayashi T, Kitamura T. Text-independent speaker identification using Gaussian mixture models based on multi-space probability distribution. [Journal Paper] *IEICE Transactions on Information & Systems, vol.E84-D, no.7, July 2001,* pp.847-55. Publisher: Inst. Electron. Inf. & Commun. Eng. Japan.
Abstract • Complete Reference

☐ 4. Ching-Tang Hsieh, You-Chuang Wang. A robust speaker identification system based on wavelet transform. [Journal Paper] *IEICE Transactions on Information & Systems, vol.E84-D, no.7, July 2001,* pp.839-46. Publisher: Inst. Electron. Inf. & Commun. Eng. Japan.
Abstract • Complete Reference

☐ 5. Li X, Mak MW, Kung SY. Robust speaker verification over the telephone by feature recuperation. [Conference Paper] *Proceedings of 2001 International Symposium on Intelligent Multimedia, Video and Speech Processing. ISIMP 2001 (IEEE Cat. No.01EX489). IEEE.* 2001, pp.433-6. Piscataway, NJ, USA.
Abstract • Complete Reference

☐ 6. Siew Chan Woo, Chee Peng Lim, Osman R. Development of a speaker recognition system using wavelets and artificial neural networks. [Conference Paper] *Proceedings of 2001 International Symposium on Intelligent Multimedia, Video and Speech Processing. ISIMP 2001 (IEEE Cat. No.01EX489). IEEE.* 2001, pp.413-16. Piscataway, NJ, USA.
Abstract • Complete Reference

☐ 7. Mak MW, Zhang WD, He MX. A new two-stage scoring normalization approach to speaker verification. [Conference Paper] *Proceedings of 2001 International Symposium on Intelligent Multimedia, Video and Speech Processing. ISIMP 2001 (IEEE Cat. No.01EX489). IEEE.* 2001, pp.107-10. Piscataway, NJ, USA.
Abstract • Complete Reference

☐ 8. Hu Guangrui, Wei Xiaodong. Improved robust speaker identification in noise using auditory properties. [Conference Paper] *Proceedings of 2001 International Symposium on Intelligent Multimedia, Video and Speech Processing. ISIMP 2001 (IEEE Cat. No.01EX489). IEEE.* 2001, pp.17-19. Piscataway, NJ, USA.
Abstract • Complete Reference

☐ 9. Hea-Kyoung Jung, Yu-Jin Kim, Jae-Ho Chung. The implementation of PFCMS using cepstrum information. [Conference Paper] *ISCAS 2001. The 2001 IEEE International Symposium on Circuits and Systems (Cat. No.01CH37196). IEEE. Part vol 2,* 2001, pp.365-8 vol 2. Piscataway, NJ, USA.
Abstract • Complete Reference

☐ 10. Zhen Bin, Wu Xihong, Liu Zhimin, Chi Huisheng. An enhanced RASTA filtering of speech. [Journal Paper] *Acta Acustica, vol.26, no.3, May 2001,* pp.252-8. Publisher: Inst. Acoust. Acad. Sinica, China.
Abstract • Complete Reference

Index →

Figure 25g: INSPEC *on EDINA using OVID search software. (Used with the permission of the Institution of Electrical Engineers, EDINA and OVID Technologies Inc.)*

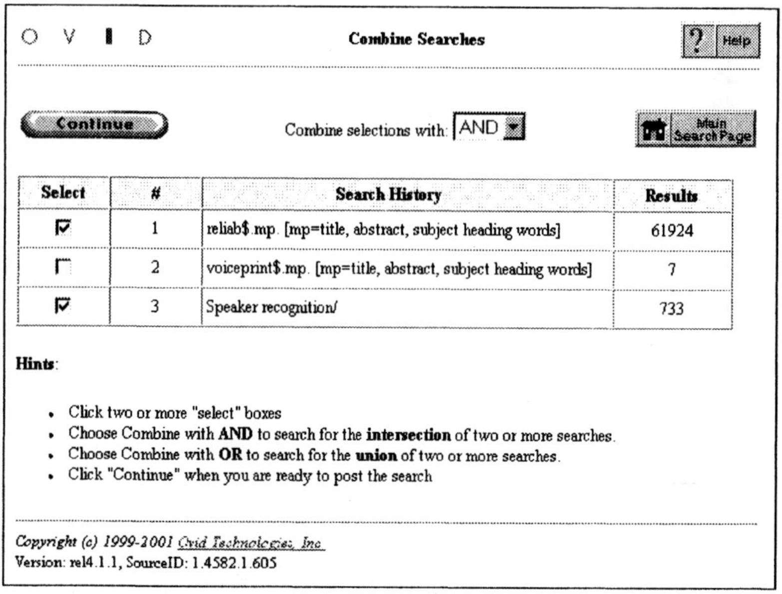

| O V ∎ D | Combine Searches | ? Help |

```
( Continue )          Combine selections with: | AND ▼ |          [⊞ Main Search Page]
```

Select	#	Search History	Results
☑	1	reliab$.mp. [mp=title, abstract, subject heading words]	61924
☐	2	voiceprint$.mp. [mp=title, abstract, subject heading words]	7
☑	3	Speaker recognition/	733

Hints:

- Click two or more "select" boxes
- Choose Combine with **AND** to search for the **intersection** of two or more searches.
- Choose Combine with **OR** to search for the **union** of two or more searches.
- Click "Continue" when you are ready to post the search

Copyright (c) 1999-2001 Ovid Technologies, Inc
Version: rel4.1.1, SourceID: 1.4582.1.605

Figure 25h: INSPEC *on* EDINA *using OVID search software. (Used with the permission of the Institution of Electrical Engineers, EDINA and OVID Technologies Inc.)*

O V I D INSPEC ? Help
<1996 to 2001 Week 31>

Author Title Journal Search Tools Combine Limit Basic Change Logoff
Fields Database

#	Search History	Results	Display
1	rehab$.mp. [mp=title, abstract, subject heading words]	61924	Display
2	voiceprint$.mp. [mp=title, abstract, subject heading words]	7	Display
3	Speaker recognition/	733	Display
4	1 and 3	30	Display

Run Saved Search   Save Search History   Delete Searches

Enter Keyword or phrase: ☑ Map Term to Subject Heading

Perform Search

Limit to:
☐ Latest Update ☐ Abstracts ☐ English Language ☐ Journal Paper
Publication Year - [ ] - [ ]

Results of your search: **1 and 3**
Citations displayed: **1-10 of 30**
Go to Record: 1

Citation Manager • Help • Logoff

Customize Display |Reset Display

☐ 1. Monrose F, Reiter MK, Qi Li, Wetzel S. Cryptographic key generation from voice [Conference Paper] *Proceedings 2001 IEEE Symposium on Security and Privacy. S&P 2001. IEEE Comput. Soc. 2001, pp.202-13. Los Alamitos, CA, USA*
Abstract • Complete Reference

☐ 2. Burileanu D, Pascalin L, Burileanu C, Puchiu M. An adaptive and fast speech detection algorithm [Conference Paper] *Text, Speech and Dialogue. Third International Workshop, TSD 2000. Proceedings (Lecture Notes in Artificial Intelligence Vol.1902). Springer-Verlag. 2000, pp.177-82. Berlin, Germany.*
Abstract • Complete Reference

☐ 3. Uchibe T, Kuroiwa S, Higuchi N. Determination of threshold for text prompted speaker verification [Journal Paper] *Transactions of the Institute of Electronics, Information & Communication Engineers D-II, vol.J83D-II, no.11, Nov. 2000, pp.2291-9. Publisher: Inst. Electron. Inf. & Commun. Eng, Japan.*
Abstract • Complete Reference

☐ 4. Damiano B, Kercel SW, Tucker RW Jr, Brown-VanHoozer SA. Recognizing a voice from its model [Conference Paper] *SMC 2000 Conference Proceedings. 2000 IEEE International Conference on Systems, Man and Cybernetics. 'Cybernetics Evolving to Systems, Humans, Organizations, and their Complex Interactions' (Cat. No.00CH37166). IEEE. Part vol.3, 2000, pp.2216-21 vol.3. Piscataway, NJ, USA.*
Abstract • Complete Reference

☐ 5. Ramachandran RP, Farrell KR. Fast pole filtering for speaker recognition [Conference Paper] *2000 IEEE International Symposium on Circuits and Systems. Emerging Technologies for the 21st Century. Proceedings (IEEE Cat No. 00CH36353). Presses Polytech. Univ. Romandes. Part vol.5, 2000, pp.49-52 vol.5. Lausanne, Switzerland.*
Abstract • Complete Reference

☐ 6. Lim CP, Woo SC, Loh AS, Osman R. Speech recognition using artificial neural networks. [Conference Paper] *Proceedings of the First International Conference on Web Information Systems Engineering. IEEE Comput. Soc. Part vol.1, 2000, pp.419-23 vol.1. Los Alamitos, CA, USA.*
Abstract • Complete Reference

☐ 7. Zhu Liu, Qian Huang. Adaptive anchor detection using online trained audio/visual model [Conference Paper] *SPIE-Int. Soc. Opt. Eng. Proceedings of Spie - the International Society for Optical Engineering, vol.3972, 2000, pp.156-67. USA.*
Abstract • Complete Reference

☐ 8. Nickel RM, Williams WJ. On local time-frequency features of speech and their employment in speaker verification. [Conference Paper] *Elsevier. Journal of the Franklin Institute, vol.337, no.4, July 2000, pp.469-81. UK.*
Abstract • Complete Reference

☐ 9. Boe L-J. Forensic voice identification in France. [Journal Paper] *Speech Communication, vol.31, no.2-3, June 2000, pp.205-24. Publisher: Elsevier, Netherlands.*
Abstract • Complete Reference

☐ 10. Cerrato L, Falcone M, Paoloni A. Subjective age estimation of telephonic voices. [Journal Paper] *Speech Communication, vol.31, no.2-3, June 2000, pp.107-12. Publisher: Elsevier, Netherlands.*
Abstract • Complete Reference

Figure 25i: INSPEC *on EDINA using OVID search software. (Used with the permission of the Institution of Electrical Engineers, EDINA and OVID Technologies Inc.)*

quently have included (or cited) the paper in their list of references. It is possible to find out who has subsequently referred to an earlier article by using a database called *Science Citation Index* or *SCI*.

Science Citation Index can be searched for articles on a particular subject in the same way as other bibliographic databases such as *MEDLINE* or *INSPEC*, but it can in addition be used to search forward in time. The basic principle behind the *Science Citation Index* rests on the fact that although more than 30,000 scientific and technical journals are published worldwide each year, most of the significant information is contained within a much smaller number.

The policy of the producers, ISI, is to index the contents of these highly rated scientific and technical journals (approximately 5,700 in 2001). Every paper in these journals is included (whatever the subject field) along with all the references or citations to publications made by the authors to previous work. The direct linkage of these earlier references to recently published papers then makes it feasible to carry out a "forward in time" search using the earlier reference as the starting-point. The search in Figures 26a to 26f was carried out using the *Science Citation Index* database on the *Web of Science* (*WoS*) service, based at the *MIMAS* data centre. This is available to universities and other higher education institutions in the UK, who have paid for subscriptions. *Science Citation Index* on *Web of Science* is also available worldwide, so if you think it would be useful to you, ask your library or information centre if it subscribes to the database.

The starting point for the search was the reference below, one of the key papers about the cloning of "Dolly the sheep":

K. H. S. Campbell, J. McWhir, W. A. Ritchie and I. Wilmut.
Sheep cloned by nuclear transfer from a cultured cell line.
Nature Volume *380* 7 March 1996 pp. 64–66.

The name of the first author, Campbell, the title of the journal, and the place of work were typed in on the General Search screen on *Web of Science*, as shown in Figure 26c. The search of the database found seven articles with K. H. S. Campbell as the first or subsequent author, the correct paper being the seventh one in the display (Figure 26d). Following the hyperlink from the title displayed the full record, with several more hyperlinks, one of which is "Times Cited" (Figure 26e). This hyperlink leads to the list in Figure 26f, showing that by the date the search was carried out, 288 papers had cited the article since it was published in 1996.

Refining a search

These examples were chosen to demonstrate the basic principles of searching bibliographic databases. Not all searches work out in practice as simply as these. Sometimes a combination of concepts produces almost no references at all. In these circumstances it is necessary to

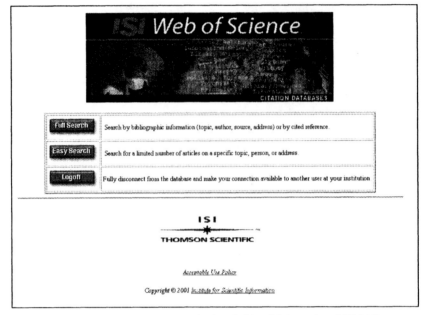

Figure 26a: Science Citation Index *(Web of Science) on* MIMAS

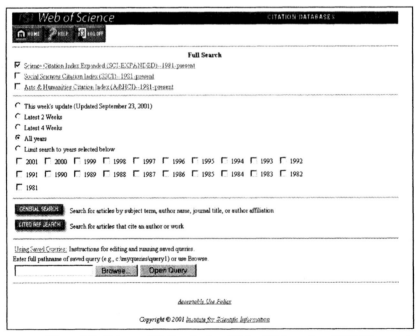

Figure 26b: Science Citation Index *(Web of Science) on* MIMAS

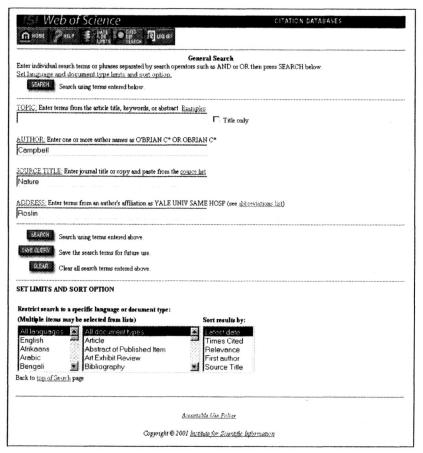

Figure 26c: Science Citation Index *(Web of Science) on* MIMAS

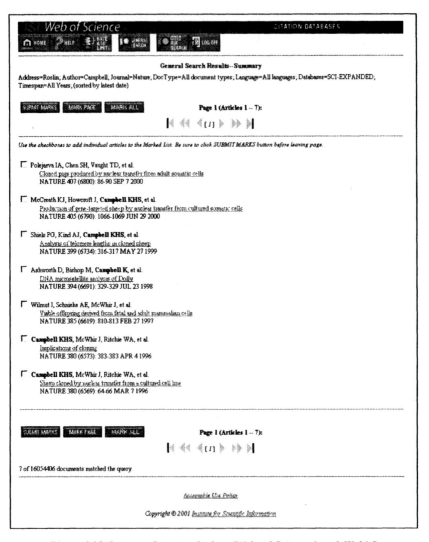

Figure 26d: Science Citation Index (Web of Science) *on* MIMAS

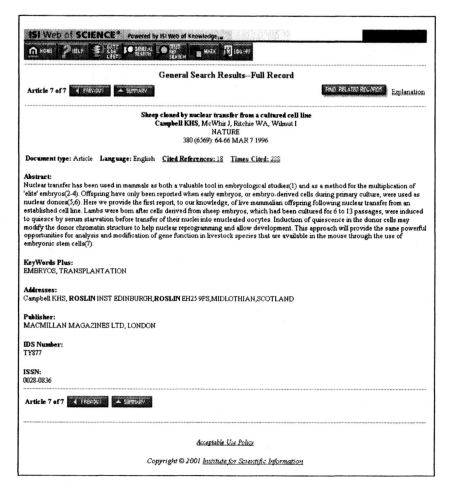

Figure 26e: Science Citation Index *(Web of Science) on* MIMAS

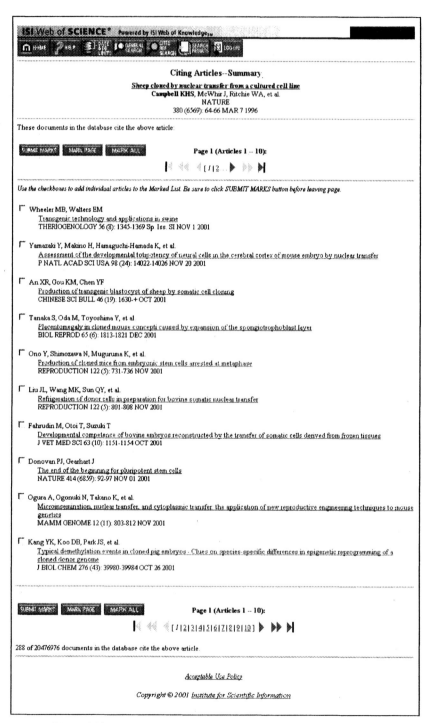

Figure 26f: Science Citation Index *(Web of Science) on* MIMAS

drop the least important concept, or widen the scope of a concept by introducing more keywords, or by using broader subject terms.

If too many references are found, then the scope of the search needs to be restricted by introducing more concepts, using narrower subject terms or reducing the number in some other way. Some popular ways of doing this include limiting the search to references less than a few years old, or restricting the references found to reviews, or by only searching for keywords in the title of the paper.

There are times, however much a search is broadened or narrowed, when the results are not what is required. This is quite a frustrating situation, particularly as people are usually sure that some work has been carried out on the subject. The first thing to do in these circumstances is to try an alternative database to the one you have been using. If this approach fails, it would be worth asking your library or information centre if it offers "mediated" searching. This type of searching involves library staff logging onto to a host system with databases that are accessed on a "pay-as-you-go basis".

The most well known of these systems is *Dialog*, with a very large number of bibliographic databases, including many specialised ones such as *Ceramic Abstracts* and *Food Science and Technology Abstracts*. The library or information unit would normally recover some of their costs by charging for the search, the cost depending on several factors, including the number of records found. Often this is paid for out of a research groups funds, and can be money well spent if it locates a few difficult to find core references.

Another situation when it is important to get professional help is in searching patent literature. The free patent databases listed in Table 2 (p. 57) are very useful orientation tools for getting an overview of what has been patented in an area. It is very important though that anyone who is seriously considering applying for a patent consults a patent agent, who will conduct exhaustive searches prior to an application being submitted.

Factual databases

In addition to bibliographic databases, there is a large range of factual databases likely to be of relevance at some point in a project. Chemists working or studying in UK universities, for example, have free access to the *Chemical Data Service* (*CDS*) (*http://cds3.dl.ac.uk/cds/*), based at the Daresbury Laboratory, part of the Central Laboratory of the Research Councils. The *Chemical Data Service* function is hosting access to a range of high-quality comprehensive databases, covering crystallography, spectroscopy, organic and physical chemistry. The

Medical Research Council support the *UK Human Genome Mapping Project Resource Centre (HGMP-RC)*. The Centre provides programs and databases in the genetics and genomics – the study of DNA sequences in the chromosomes of organisms (*http://www.hgmp.mrc.ac.uk/*).

In the technical area, one of the best known services is *ESDU (Engineering Sciences Data Unit) International* at *http://www.esdu.com/*. ESDU, originally established by the Royal Aeronautical Society in 1940, provides validated engineering design data, methods and software for engineers. ESDU is now a commercial enterprise, charging for its services, but supported by independent committees of experts from industry, research organisations and universities worldwide.

CDS, HGMP-RC and *ESDU* provide access to large, well-used databases, but there are many more that cannot be covered here. It is worth keeping a watch in the newsletters and journals of specialist subject fields for publicity about these services.

Summary

- Find out which bibliographic databases are available via your library or information centre.

- When choosing a bibliographic database to search, look at the way the subject is emphasised, and check the list of journals indexed for ones relevant to your subject field.

- Before starting a search, determine its subject content as specifically as possible and include any synonyms known to you.

- Be wary of any search which produces no references – it may be due to misspelling a keyword.

- Check any really important references in *Science Citation Index* on *Web of Science* to see if these have subsequently been cited by other authors.

- If you are having difficulty finding references, ask your library or information service if there are any specialised bibliographic databases which could be searched for a fee.

Chapter 5

Obtaining and organising information

Having carried out a search using a bibliographic database such as *Medline* or *INSPEC*, you will almost certainly have found some references — maybe only four or five but possibly 50 or more. The first step is to evaluate these, deciding which are sufficiently relevant to make it worthwhile obtaining in full text, and which are only of fringe interest. The abstracts are your main tool in making this assessment. Although it may seem obvious, it is also useful to check that the article is written in English or another language that you understand.

Many of the references found during a search will be journal articles. Although colleagues might be able to supply you with the occasional item, in most instances you will have to rely on the resources of your library or information centre. Just as with a reference to a book, the holdings of your library or information centre should be checked to see if it is available – either as a printed item or in electronic format. People familiar with a particular library often forget to do this, assuming that they are familiar with everything to which the organisation subscribes.

Electronic journals

If the journal is in stock as a printed publication, this will be displayed in the catalogue, with the location so you can find the item on the shelves. The situation with journals published in electronic format is slightly more complicated. Some libraries include all the titles of the electronic journals to which they subscribe in their catalogue, making this a "one-stop shop" for checking purposes. Other libraries keep the list of electronic journals separate from the catalogue. What this means in practice is that it may be necessary to make two checks – the main library catalogue and the separate list of electronic journals – to be certain whether or not a title is available.

Where there is a subscription to an electronic journal, the library catalogue or list of titles will give the Web address. If you are using a Web catalogue from an office or lab this could be a hyperlink, so that you can click on this to get to the Web site immediately. If you are working in a library itself, the catalogue link may not be live, and you will need to record the Web address and access the site on a different workstation. Although this may be irritating, there is a sound reason for the practice – with a limited number of workstations available, a library cannot afford to have the terminals occupied for long spells of time by users who may be surfing the Internet.

The Web address that is given for a title may be either for:

• the Web site of the publisher of the journal
• an "aggregator", an organisation giving a single point of access to a large number of electronic journals.

In either case, the Web address provided may point specifically to the actual journal title itself, or to the home page of the publisher's or aggregator's Web site.

Well-known aggregators include *ingenta Journals, SwetsnetNavigator,* and *EBSCO Online.* As the screen display from *ingenta Journals* in Figure 27 shows, the JOURNAL SEARCH option can be used to find a title, either directly by typing in the name of the journal or by browsing through an alphabetical list.

Figure 27: ingenta Journals. *(Used with the permission of ingenta plc.)*

Aggregators and publishers check whether a subscription exists by either:

- asking the user to enter a username and password
- by ensuring that the request to view an article comes from a computer with a known IP (Internet Protocol) address, previously supplied by the organisation paying for the journal.

This often means that if you contact the Web site from a computer at your place of work, you should be able to go directly to the article, as the IP address for the site will be recognised by the publisher or aggregator. If you want to work from home or another location away from the organisation itself, then you will need a username and password from your library or information unit, as the system will not recognise the workstation.

Linking from other sources

Another route for obtaining articles is via linking from bibliographic databases or the references included in a paper. If you use *PubMed*, for instance, you may see a hyperlink from the reference to the full text of the article. A link on screen connects to the journal publisher's Web site. Some articles can be displayed free of charge, though these are a minority in number. Other links lead to journal Web sites, where you can display the full text of the article if your library has paid for a subscription.

Other service providers also provide linking facilities, although the way these are implemented varies. The *Science Citation Index* database on *Web of Science* at *MIMAS*, for example, offers the facility of linking to library catalogues, to enable someone to check if a paper copy of a journal subscription exists. Whether this facility is available to a user at a particular institution will depend on whether the library or information centre has been able to implement the feature. Links from references at the end of a paper to the cited article are also gradually becoming more common. The point to be aware of is that links are worth following when you come across them, but are not guaranteed to provide "free" access to the full text of an article.

Viewing articles on screen

To be able to display the full text of a journal article on screen, a computer must be equipped with suitable viewing software. The main software package used by publishers is Adobe Acrobat, which displays articles in a delivery format known as PDF (Portable Document Format). Using PDF preserves the original appearance and page layout – it means that if both an electronic and print version of a journal is published, articles look the same on screen as they do on paper. The Adobe Acrobat Reader software, which is free to install on a compu-

ter, can be downloaded from the Adobe web site at *http://www.adobe.com/*
.

Some publishers also make their articles available in HTML format as a Web page. Although the electronic version of an article will not be a facsimile of the printed copy, the hyperlinks can be useful in jumping from one section of the article to another, or sometimes to related references. Another advantage of articles in HTML format is that the figures and illustrations can be expanded to be viewed in greater detail.

Authors' copies

Sometimes it is possible to get hold of papers from the author's own Web pages, mentioned in Chapter 1. The papers may be pre-publication drafts, the actual format and layout of the information varying from the final printed or electronic version. With a very recently published paper, you could also try asking the author directly for an off-print. At publication, most journals either give or sell authors' copies, known as off-prints or reprints, to distribute themselves. Some of these are immediately given to colleagues; the remainder are sent out to anyone expressing an interest in the work. Requesting off-prints directly from authors, although sometimes slow, is particularly useful where a paper contains photographs which do not copy well.

E-print archives

Alternatively the e-print archives or servers mentioned in Chapter 1 are an obvious source to try, although it should be remembered that the papers may not have been formally published (i.e. peer reviewed) as would be the case with journals. Useful sites include:

- *arc – http://arc.cs.odu.edu/*. This is a search engine for finding e-prints across a range of servers.
- *arXiv – http://www.arxiv.org*. The largest e-print archive, with over 155,000 in physics, mathematics, computer science and non-linear systems.
- *BioMed Central – http://www.biomedcentral.com/*. This is primarily a collection of peer-reviewed journals in biology and medicine, published free of charge on the Internet.
- *The Chemistry Preprint Server – http://www.chemweb.com/*. Access is free but users need to register as ChemWeb members first.
- *CogPrints – http://cogprints.soton.ac.uk/*. A collection covering psychology, neuroscience and linguistics, plus some areas in computer science, biology and philosophy.

- *HighWire Press – http://highwire.stanford.edu/*. A very large site of full text articles from many major journals in the biomedical and life sciences subject field.

- *NASA Astrophysics Data System – http://ukads.nottingham.ac.uk*. Like *HighWire*, this contains a very large number of articles from published journals. The subject field's covered include astronomical and planetary sciences, solar physics, plus some areas of physics and instrumentation.

- *The PrePrint Network – http://www.osti.gov/preprint/*. Developed by the US Department of Energy, the *Network* aims at being a one-stop shop for links to a whole range of pre-print servers in scientific and technical fields.

Other libraries

Another option is to check if the journal or book is in stock at another library nearby. Most university library catalogues are easily accessed via the Internet, using the Library OPACS in HE Web page at *NISS (National Information Services and Systems)* shown in Figure 28 as a starting point (*http://www.niss.ac.uk/lis/opacs.html*). This Web page provides links to Library OPACS (online public access catalogues) by region and alphabetically. It includes the catalogues of virtually all UK universities, and a range of other institutions such as the Royal Society of Chemistry, and the Royal Greenwich Observatory, as well as the British Library Public Catalogue and *COPAC*, mentioned in Chapter 3.

Other libraries will not lend directly to non-members, but you might be able to use the item on the premises. If so, this can be a quick way of getting hold of a paper needed urgently. Before actually visiting another library though, do check first to see whether there are any entry conditions – many universities now require identification from outsiders, and may allow visits only during vacations, for instance.

An increasing number of university libraries participate in reciprocal-borrowing schemes. These are schemes set up to enable certain users to have access rights and to borrow books from other local institutions. A well-known one is the M25 Access and Borrowing Scheme, in which nearly 40 universities and other higher education institutions in the London area participate. Other schemes have been set up in the Manchester and the West Midlands regions. It is worth asking if there is anything similar in your area that you would be eligible to join.

Interlibrary loan

Almost inevitably some of the references you need will not be available either via your library or through one of the other channels outlined

niss

Library OPACs in HE

UK OPACs - in Alphabetical Order

Some OPACs require a logon id, username and/or password - and some include this information on the screens that users
see when they access the catalogue. Where this information is not immediately apparent on the OPAC screens themselves,
we have added it to the description field in the OPAC's [*Info*] page.

Higher Education Institutions

- Aberdeen, University of [*Info*]
- Abertay Dundee, University of [*Info*]
- Aberystwyth, University of Wales [*Info*]
- Anglia Polytechnic University [*Info*]
- Aston University [*Info*]
- Bangor, University of Wales [*Info*]
- Bath, University of [*Info*]
- Bath Spa University College [*Info*]
- Bell College, Hamilton [*Info*]
- Birkbeck College, University of London [*Info*]
- Birmingham, University of [*Info*]
- Bolton Institute of Higher Education [*Info*]
- Bournemouth University [*Info*]
- Bradford, University of [*Info*]
- Brighton, University of [*Info*]
- Bristol, University of [*Info*]
- British Library of Political and Economic Science, University of London [*Info*]
- Brunel University, West London [*Info*]
- Buckingham, University of [*Info*]
- Cambridge, University of [*Info*]
- Canterbury Christ Church University College [*Info*]
- Cardiff, University of Wales [*Info*]
- Central England, University of [*Info*]
- Central Lancashire, University of [*Info*]
- Central School of Speech and Drama [*Info*] (The catalogue is not available at present.)
- Chester College [*Info*]
- City University [*Info*]
- College of Medicine, University of Wales [*Info*]
- Coventry University [*Info*]
- Cranfield University [*Info*]
- Dartington College of Arts [*Info*]
- De Montfort University [*Info*]
- Derby, University of [*Info*]
- Dundee, University of [*Info*]
- Durham, University of [*Info*]
- East Anglia, University of [*Info*]
- East London, University of [*Info*]
- Edge Hill College [*Info*]
- Edinburgh College of Art [*Info*]
- Edinburgh, University of [*Info*]
- Essex, University of [*Info*]
- Exeter, University of [*Info*]
- Girton College, Cambridge [*Info*]
- Glamorgan, University of [*Info*]
- Glasgow, University of [*Info*] (includes the former St Andrew's College)
- Glasgow Caledonian University [*Info*]
- Glasgow School of Art [*Info*]
- Gloucestershire, University of (formerly Cheltenham & Gloucester College of HE) [*Info*]
- Goldsmith's College, University of London [*Info*]
- Greenwich, University of [*Info*]
- Harper Adams University College [*Info*]
- Heriot-Watt University [*Info*]

Figure 28: NISS Library OPACS in HE

above, and will have to be obtained elsewhere. Although libraries will consider buying publications needed by readers, it is generally faster to obtain a book or a photocopy of an article from another library, a procedure known as interlibrary loan (ILL), or alternatively by its newer name of "document delivery". British researchers are fortunate in that a sophisticated interlibrary loan service has been developed in the UK. The main source is the Document Supply Centre (DSC) belonging to the British Library. Basically this is a warehouse at Boston Spa in Yorkshire providing a fast, comprehensive service supplying copies of journal articles and loans of books.

You will almost certainly be asked to fill in a form or card, such as the one in Figure 29, for each publication you want. Note that the form asks for the source of the reference. This is a common precaution against inaccuracies: if the reference is wrong it may still be possible to track down the correct publication from the original source.

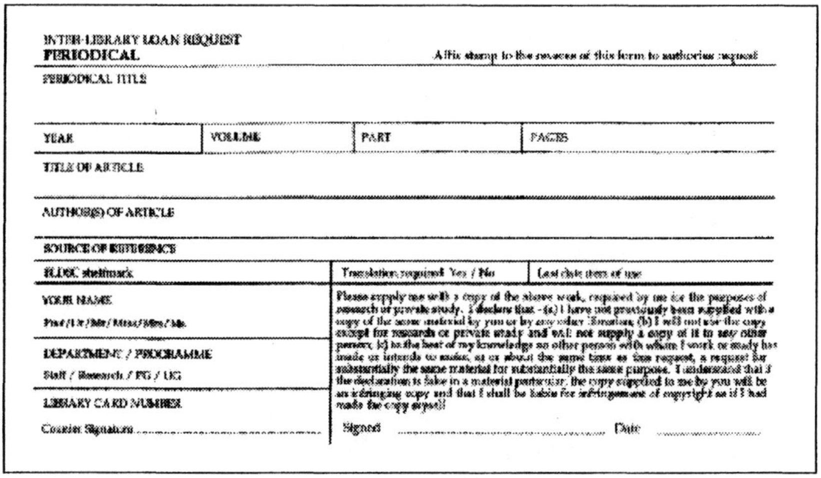
INTER-LIBRARY LOAN REQUEST
PERIODICAL
Affix stamp to the reverse of this form to authorise request
PERIODICAL TITLE
YEAR | VOLUME | PART | PAGES
TITLE OF ARTICLE
AUTHOR(S) OF ARTICLE
SOURCE OF REFERENCE
BLDSC shelfmark | Translation required: Yes / No | Last date item of use
YOUR NAME
DEPARTMENT / PROGRAMME
Staff / Research / PG / UG
LIBRARY CARD NUMBER
Counter Signature
Signed | Date

Figure 29: Interlibrary loan request card

One aspect about interlibrary loans which ought to be mentioned is that there is a cost to libraries and information units in obtaining material, whether from the Document Supply Centre or other organisations. Although most libraries do not directly charge their users, limited budgets mean that demand is likely to be controlled in some way, such as by using vouchers, or by setting an upper limit on the number of requests which can be made at any one time. Such restrictions are necessary evils, but they can create a negative impression amongst readers. No library would want you to be deterred from requesting items important for your work, so do ask if you need help.

Using the interlibrary loan service is a reliable, convenient way of getting hold of publications, but there will be a wait of a few days or more before the material arrives. For the majority of requests this delay, though not ideal, is generally acceptable. If you want an article, book or other publication urgently, you will have to try other methods of supply. The Document Supply Centre operates an Urgent Action Service; although more expensive than the normal service, this guarantees that if a specially requested item is in stock, it will be sent off the same day either by fax, mail, courier, or Aerial – an electronic document-delivery service.

Copyright legislation

This outline would not be complete without mentioning copyright legislation. This aims to keep a balance between the rights of authors and publishers to obtain a fair return for their work and the right of the public to have access to knowledge. One aspect of copyright legislation of particular significance to scientific, technical and medical researchers is that concerning the photocopying of papers from journals. In the UK, the 1956 Copyright Act allowed single copies of articles required for research or private study to be made from journals without payment of royalties. This position was not changed when new legislation, the Copyright, Designs and Patents Act, was passed in 1988. This Act however does not permit multiple copying of articles without payment, or copying more than one article from a journal issue. In these circumstances a library can use the "Copyright Fee Paid Copy Service" from the Document Supply Centre to obtain the articles. This service is more expensive though, because it includes a copyright fee, passed on by the Copyright Licensing Agency, an organisation responsible for distributing the charges to the rights' holders worldwide.

Another aspect of copyright legislation affecting researchers is that relating to downloading. Downloading is the transfer and storage of references from a database to a computer – its applications are out-lined in the next section. The 1988 Copyright, Designs and Patents Act does not specifically mention downloading. In practice this is usually covered by the licensing agreements set by the producers, and signed by library or information units when they subscribe to the databases. Many will allow users to download references to set up a personal file of the kind described below, but prohibit the transfer in any way to third parties, such as researchers in other universities or companies.

Organising personal collections

Most students and researchers will have experienced the problem of trying to find a particular reference or piece of information they know to be in their own personal literature collection and the subsequent irritation if the search proves fruitless. It is obviously impossible to set exact limits, but above a certain size an individual collection kept in no particular order will tend to become unwieldy. Added to this is the fact that most researchers' literature collections are really mixtures of the complete texts of papers in the form of photocopies and print-outs, and references to some material not actually in their possession: books, conferences and the like. Many of these references are likely to be on odd scraps of paper, backs of envelopes, and so on.

Laying down hard-and-fast rules about how to organise a literature collection would obviously be inappropriate. People with photographic memories may be quite happy with a few hundred papers in no particular order, whereas those who like order and tidiness could probably not tolerate a random pile of photocopies and reports. What we can do is to give some general guidelines and point to some current solutions which are likely to make the task easier.

The simplest solution is to depend on the physical organisation of the material alone, arranging papers according to fairly specific subject areas. Information for which you have the reference only but no original would have to be filed separately, preferably using the same subject groups. Having more than one place to look can be a nuisance: it is easy to overlook one of them, and you would have to rely on memory to find papers by particular authors. The system does have the great advantage of needing little time or effort to set up and maintain; organising and indexing a personal collection will inevitably be low down on a list of priorities when time is short.

Personal bibliographic software

These types of manual systems are clearly best suited to small personal collections, used by one individual. Collections which are likely to reach a reasonably large size, or are shared between a group of people, would benefit from a more organised system using a computer. It is possible to use a general database management system such as Microsoft Access. There is also a range of software packages available – sometimes referred to as Personal Bibliographic Managers (PBMs) – specifically designed for storing, indexing and outputting a database of references. Well-known applications include EndNote, ProCite, Research Manager, Citation, Bookends Plus, Biblioscape and Papyrus.

Using a PBM software package can offer considerable advantages over a manual collection of references, but it is important to be clear what it can do, as establishing and maintaining a reasonable database requires planning and effort. The benefits can include:

- The ability to transfer or import records from other databases. A PBM software package should provide facilities for importing references from popular bibliographic databases into the appropriate format for the personal database, a useful, time-saving practice.

- Improved searching facilities compared with a manual system. A computerised system can search all the separate parts of a reference, including all the words in the title and any keywords or indexing terms added to the reference by the individual setting up the database.

- The facility to insert references into a paper as it is being written. This feature – "Cite While You Write" as it has been called – is made feasible by the close integration of PBMs with word-processing packages.

- Formatting of references in different styles. When a paper is submitted for publication to a journal, the editors will ask for the references to be set out according to a specific layout or format. With a PBM system it is possible to extract references from a database and have these references formatted by the package into the layout required by a specific journal.

If a decision is made to set up a database, then the next step is to choose the software. As mentioned, there are a range of software packages around which could be used for this purpose. Whatever the software, however, it will need to be able to carry out certain basic functions. These functions fall into the following categories.

Creating a record format

Before a reference can be entered into a computer, a suitable record format or data structure must exist. A record format for a reference would normally consist of a number of separate parts or fields. Each field would store a part of the reference, so, for example, there would be an author field, a title field, an abstract field and so on. With general database packages, users would have to set up their own record formats, making their own decisions about which fields to include, how long they should be and what they should be called. A PBM system should provide predefined record formats or templates. Endnote, for example, has 16 predefined work forms (called Reference Types), covering different material formats such as books, journal articles, patents and electronic sources.

The fields in a record can be either fixed or variable lengths. With variable-length fields, the size can vary from record to record, depending on the information it contains. A title such as *"Ice-cover influence in near-field mixing in dune-bed channel: numerical simulation"*, for example, would require a much longer field than a title such as *"Ice thrust in reservoirs"*.

Fields of fixed length, on the other hand, always consist of the same number of characters and spaces regardless of their contents. For example, a fixed-length field for a title might be 60 characters in length. This would be sufficient to store the second title but not the first. Variable-length fields are preferable for collections of references because of the wide variation in length of titles and abstracts, but not all packages provide such a feature.

Adding new records

While typing in references is obviously a standard feature, it can be a tedious and error-prone process. It often entails the user manually changing the format of the reference from that used by the bibliographic database, as there is no standard way of setting out references. One database may display the author first, where another may choose the title as the first part or field of the record. Similarly there are different ways of setting out the elements and order of the reference – the year of publication, volume and page numbers. A PBM package may provide files, known as filters, which convert or translate the reference from the formats used by bibliographic databases to the style used in the personal collection. A separate filter is needed for each bibliographic database. Filters for popular databases would normally be included in the package.

Z39.50 Searching

Z39.50 is an international standard or protocol enabling the software on one computer to search a database on another system, provided that this is also "Z39.50 compliant". What this means in practice is that a bibliographic database can be searched using the software application's own search interface, not the one provided by the supplier or service provider. Some PBM packages offer Z39.50 searching facilities – ones that do include EndNote, Reference Manager and ProCite, listed in the Products section at the end of this chapter.

The advantage of Z39.50 searching is that users can avoid having to become familiar with a whole range of interfaces on different bibliographic databases. In addition a Z39.50 searching facility eliminates the need to use import filters when adding the references retrieved during a search to a personal database – the PBM software will convert the data without any intervention. However not all bibliographic databases are Z39.50 compliant. There can also be a downside in that a Z39.50 interface may not be able to match the sophisticated search facilities available on many bibliographic databases.

Indexing

For anyone setting up a personal database, the question arises of whether it is going to be worth adding extra keywords or indexing terms to each reference. The article mentioned previously (*"Ice-cover influence in near-field mixing in dune-bed channel: numerical simulation"*) is also concerned with the transportation of a contaminant, although this is not specifically mentioned in the title. If only the title and journal details are entered into the database, this reference will not be retrieved when the computer is instructed to look for contaminant. Often a researcher is interested in a paper only because a particular method has been used; this is also very unlikely to be mentioned in the title. These types of problems can be avoided by the inclusion of keywords or indexing terms for each reference. If an abstract is also included as part of a reference, then the need to include indexing terms may not be quite so great – if the title does not mention a certain topic, it could appear in the abstract. However, there can be no certainty that an abstract will cover all aspects of a paper. The only way to be sure of this is to include these aspects as indexing terms.

Some practical points to note for anyone adding indexing terms to references are:

- The indexing terms used to describe a reference should be as specific as possible. Indexing references generally rather than specifically can mean retrieving many items at each search. If items are indexed exactly it is easy, if nothing is found using a specific word, to broaden the search to more general words or phrases.

- It is important to be as consistent as possible when choosing indexing terms, for example, always using the term *reservoirs* rather than sometimes *reservoirs* and sometimes *reservoir*. The way authors cite their names can also vary, for example *P. A. Lambert* or *Peter A. Lambert;* if one form of name is chosen and kept to, it can make searching much easier. Some software packages will enable the creation of authority lists – these are indexes of the words which have previously been used as authors, keywords or journal titles – and can be used to help the user be consistent.

Searching and sorting

The capability to search the database for specific references is obviously a vital feature of this type of software package. Boolean logic – "AND", "OR" and "NOT" – searching should be available, as well as a truncation facility to find different word endings. Sorting of records into different sequences should also be a standard feature. *ProCite*, for example, provides preconfigured sorts such as author/title/date, but it is also possible for users to define their own sequence.

Output

In a personal database there will be a need for two different types of output. First is the display and printing out of a few references retrieved from the database for personal use. Since the format or layout will be of no particular importance, these can be printed out directly. The second type of output is a list of references to accompany the publication of a paper. As mentioned previously, the editors of journals usually require references to be set out or formatted to a particular style. Some, for example, require the author's name to be followed by the year of publication, as in the reference below:

> Tan, C A, Sinha, S K, and Ettema, R (1999) Ice-cover influence in near-field mixing in dune-bed channel: numerical simulation. *Journal of Cold Regions Engineering* **13** 1-20.

Others specify that the author's name is to be followed by the title of the paper, then the journal details:

> Tan, C. A., Sinha, S. K., and Ettema, R. Ice-cover influence in near-field mixing in dune-bed channel: numerical simulation. *Journal of Cold Regions Engineering* **13**(1) March 1999 1-20.

Unfortunately, since there is little standardisation of practice there are numerous different styles in use. The PBM packages aim to meet this need. *EndNote*, for example, provides over 500 different output format styles for journals published in all fields of science, engineering and medicine. The packages also provide the facility for someone to define their own format or layout, if the one needed is not present.

Another aspect of output is the seamless interface with a word-processing application – the "Cite While You Write" facility mentioned earlier. Not all packages provide this but where it is available it is a very useful feature. *EndNote*, for instance, has an extra piece of software called the "Add-in", which appears above the Tools Menu on screen. This allows the user to switch between the two packages, inserting references while writing a paper.

Products

There are, as stated earlier, a fairly large number of software packages which could be used to set up a personal database management system. The ones mentioned here are (at the time of writing) amongst the main packages in use for both individual and group literature collections.

Biblioscape
CG Information
740 Granbury Way
Alpharetta
GA 30022
USA
Email: *sales@biblioscape.com*
http://www.biblioscape.com/

Bookends Plus
Sonny Software
8903 Seneca Lane
Bethesda
MD 20817
USA
Email: *support@sonnysoftware.com*
http://www.sonnysoftware.com/

Citation
Oberon Development
147 East Oakland Avenue
Columbus
OH 43201
USA
Email: *sales@oberon-res.com*
http://www.citationonline.net/

EndNote
ISI ResearchSoft
800 Jones Street
Berkeley
CA 94170
USA
Email: *sales@isiresearchsoft.com*
http://www.isiresearchsoft.com/

Papyrus
Research Software Design™
617 SW Hume Street
Portland
OR 97219-4458
USA
Email: *info@ResearchSoftwareDesign.com*
http://www.researchsoftwaredesign.com/

ProCite
ISI ResearchSoft
800 Jones Street
Berkeley
CA 94710
USA
Email: *sales@isiresearchsoft.com*
http://www.isiresearchsoft.com/

Reference Manager
ISI ResearchSoft
800 Jones Street
Berkeley
CA 94710
USA
Email: *sales@isiresearchsoft.com*
http://www.isiresearchsoft.com/

Some organisations take out a site licence to a specific package. In the UK, Chest (Combined Higher Education Software Team) at *http://www.chest.ac.uk* also offers deals on certain packages.

Summary

- Remember to check the catalogue (and if necessary the list of electronic journals) to see which titles are available via your library or information centre.

- Use the interlibrary loan service to get hold of references which are not available locally. Alternatively, try e-print servers or authors' Web sites for drafts of papers.

- If the references are needed urgently, ask the library or information centre staff if there are any special services available.

- If not, check to see if you could use the item in another local library.

- Give some thought at the beginning of your project as to how your literature collection would best be organised.

Chapter 6

Keeping up to date

Having found and evaluated the information in your subject field, the next step is to make sure you keep up to date with current developments. You do have certain advantages in this respect: you should know the field well enough to be able to be fairly selective in what you read, and you should also have a good idea of which individuals and journals are likely to publish relevant information. The main difficulty you are likely to face will be lack of time to read all the information available: the actual process of finding the information is relatively simple.

There are really two different ways of keeping up to date. One is to go to meetings at which new techniques and developments are being discussed, and to supplement these with news and tips from colleagues; obviously most of the information picked up in this way will be verbal, rather than written, in form. The second way is to scan relevant journals, lists of new books and so on – that is, make use of published information. In practice, of course, these two methods complement one another, with most people using a mixture of both.

Verbal information

Most researchers are delighted to discuss the latest developments in their fields with interested colleagues. You can save yourself a great deal of time and effort in searching for information by discussing your problem with someone else. It is worth contacting a person who, for example, might have published recently in your field of interest. The informal atmosphere at a conference provides an ideal opportunity for what could well prove to be a valuable discussion. You might be made aware of a paper or technique your own search had missed, perhaps in a separate area of research, which could be applied to your own problem. You might also learn about things to avoid, such as experiments which failed and will never be published. Even allowing for some understandable reluctance to release information not yet published, you can often get ahead of the game by learning of a forthcoming paper "in press".

Information picked up at conferences and from colleagues and so on is very useful but it obviously cannot be depended upon totally. It might be inaccurate – there will have been no screening process to compare with the refereeing that takes place when papers are submitted to journals. Since the information is not acquired systematically, it would be very easy to miss something important. It is necessary, therefore, to supplement this verbally acquired knowledge with newly published information.

New books

As you would expect, the WWW has made it easy to find out what new books are available in a subject field. Virtually all publishers have their own Web sites, which can be scanned as the need arises. Rather than just depend on infrequent checks of sites, though, you could ask to be sent regular emails of new books in a specific subject category, for example the service offered by Prentice Hall, a large scientific and technical publisher (Figure 30). A list of Web links for major publishers and bookshops can be found on the *NISS* site at *http://www.niss.ac.uk/lis/ bookshops.html*, as shown in Figure 31. In addition there are the booksellers' Web sites, with the obvious candidate being Amazon at *http:// www.amazon.co.uk*. It also offers a regular email service of information on new books, though the categories are currently broad – for instance "Science" and "Computers – Networking and OS".

Mailing Lists

Prentice Hall periodically e-mails information about new titles through the use of electronic mailing lists. We maintain a large number of lists, organized by subject/category so that our mailings can be more focused and target your requests and areas of interest directly.

You may sign up for individual lists—or multiple lists at simultaneously. You may also remove yourself from any/all Prentice Hall electronic mailing lists that you've subscribed to previously through this section of the site.

Once you've selected an area of interest from the list below, you will be able to:

- **subscribe** to one or more lists that interest you
- **remove** your name (unsubscribe) from one or more lists

Areas of interest:

- Business
- Education, Career & Technology
- Engineering, Science, and Math
- Humanities and Social Science
- Professional and Technical Reference

Figure 30: Prentice Hall electronic mailing list

Bookshops and Publishers

For links to bookshops and publishers offering online catalogue and how-to-order information for mainly printed material. Other sections offer links to electronic versions of texts, to sources dealing specifically with audiobooks, to sources of texts in languages other than English, to information about book fairs and awards, and to miscellaneous related resources (such as "Books In Print" and suppliers of videos).

Booksellers, bookshops and publishers

- UK and Ireland University Press sites.

- AcqWeb's Directory of Publishers and Vendors - links to over 1,000 publishers and booksellers world-wide (maintained at Vanderbilt University). [*Info*]
- Academic Press - publisher and bookseller. [*Info*]
- Addison Wesley Longman - an educational publishing company. [*Info*]
- Amazon.co.uk - the UK site for the large general online bookstore. [*Info*]
  Or try the original Amazon.com US site. [*Info*]
- Antiquarian Booksellers' Association of America - information about ABAA and online catalogues from ABAA dealers and booksellers. [*Info*]
- Antiquarian Books in Scandinavia - access to a combined database of approximately 40 antiquarian bookshops. [*Info*]
- arts-books.com - a specialist dance and performing arts bookseller (formerly Dancebase). [*Info*]
- Ashgate - humanities and social sciences publisher. [*Info*]
- Attic Press - publisher specializing in Irish/Women's Studies, history and practical reference books by, for and about women with an international and Irish profile. [*Info*]
- Bagchee Associates - a book dealer specialising in Indian academic books. [*Info*]
- Blackwell Publishers - covering humanities, social sciences and business titles. [*Info*]
- Blackwell's Online Bookshop - bookseller specializing in scholarly, technical and research titles. [*Info*]
- BOL - the UK site of a large general online bookstore, a subsidiary of Bertelsmann. [*Info*]
- The Book Pl@ce - a UK online bookstore from Hammicks Bookshops and Book Data. [*Info*]
- Book Stacks Unlimited - online bookstore and readers' conference system in Cleveland, USA. [*Info*]
- Bookstore - at the University of California. Users can browse the database, consult best seller lists and order books online. [*Info*]
- BookWorld Publications - a specialist legal publisher with a (Central and East) European focus. [*Info*]
- Bowker - R.R.Bowker, publisher of reference works for library, publishing and bookselling professionals. [*Info*]
- Butterworths - a law and tax publisher in the UK. [*Info*]
- Carfax Publishing Ltd - a UK publisher specialising in journals. [*Info*]
- Castle Bookshop Web Site - a specialist bookseller dealing mainly in archaeology, local history, architecture, Wales, Celtic Studies and linguistics. [*Info*]
- Chadwyck-Healey - an international group of publishing companies. [*Info*]
- Chambers Harrap - a UK publisher of dictionaries and reference works. [*Info*]
- Channel Tunnel Publications - details about a range of publications on the Channel Tunnel and related subjects. [*Info*]
- Council of Europe Publishing - for titles in international and european law, human rights, constitutional and administrative law, and other fields of activity of the Council of Europe. [*Info*]
- countrybookstore.co.uk - a general bookseller in the UK offering discounted prices on all titles. [*Info*]
- CRC Press LLC - publisher in science, technology and professional subjects (includes Chapman & Hall). [*Info*]
- Crown House Publishing - for titles in psychology, personal growth, stress management, business and health. [*Info*]
- Dewi Lewis Publishing - a UK publisher specialising in photography, visual arts and fiction. [*Info*]

Figure 31: NISS *bookshops and publishers*

Scanning journals

Keeping up to date with new work published in journals is obviously of vital importance in the scientific, technical and medical fields. One popular and long established way of doing this is to pick out a handful of the most relevant journals – anything between six and twelve in number – and make certain that you check these systematically. One or two of these you may receive regularly as part of a society membership, a few might be subscribed to by your research group or department and some should be available in your library or information unit. Some journals are likely to be accessible to you electronically, and others available as printed copies, so that it will be necessary to remember to check both formats.

Electronic tables of contents alerting services

Browsing through the 10 or 12 most central journals in your subject field will help to pick up a good number of the most relevant papers being published. Inevitably though a fair number of interesting ones will be published in journals on the fringes of your subject field. How can you find out about these papers? What can you do about those journals you want to scan regularly but to which your library does not subscribe? One way is to use electronic tables of contents alerting services, which can make the task of staying up to date much easier and simpler.

Though the name may sound a bit off-putting to newcomers, these services are one of the most useful tools available to researchers. The principle is very simple – the service will alert you by email of the tables of contents of selected journals, every time new issues are published. There is no need to remember to log in every so often to see what has just been published; once you have set up a profile of your interests, the information is sent regularly to your computer, without any further action on your behalf.

Electronic tables of contents alerting services – or ETOCs as they are often referred to – are basically available via two routes:

- *Individual journal publishers.* You can for instance "sign up" or register with some major scientific, technical and medical publishers such as Academic Press, Wiley-Interscience and Springer-Verlag free of charge. Many publishers provide electronic tables of contents services, whether or not your library has subscriptions to any of their journals. If the publisher is sufficiently large or its journals fit your subject interests closely, then this type of service could fit the bill. Although the services are free, the downside is that you would need to set up a profile with each publisher who has journals relevant to your subject interests.

- *Combination of publishers.* An alternative is to use a service combining the contents pages of journals from many different publishers, so that you only register once. There are several of these types of services available – one of the major ones is *Zetoc* at *http://zetoc.mimas.ac.uk*, produced by the British Library, and provided by *MIMAS*, one of the the data centres mentioned in Chapter 4. *Zetoc* includes around 20,000 current journals and 16,000 conferences per year in its database. Since it covers the time span from 1993 to the present, the database can be used in the normal way for retrospective searching. It is though particularly useful for its current-awareness facility, known as *Zetoc Alert*. As Figure 32 shows, a *Zetoc Alert* can be set up either by selecting specific journal names or by choosing titles from a subject list – a very useful approach for anyone new to the area. Another service that you may come across includes *Inside Alert* (*http://www.bl.uk/*), also produced by the British Library. One point to mention about these services is that they do not include abstracts, so a decision on whether it is worth obtaining a paper has to be based on the title and the name of the author alone. One service which does include abstracts is *Current Contents* (*http://www.isinet.com/isi*), produced by ISI, the publishers of *Science Citation Index*. *Current Contents* is a long-established service, widely used in industry and government as well as academic settings.

You would normally expect ETOC services from individual publishers to be free of charge, but other services are fee based in some form or other – either paid for directly by a research group or company or as an entitlement because of the organisation's status. *Zetoc*, for example, is currently free to use if you are a student, researcher or member of staff at a further education college or university in the UK, as the service is paid for by JISC. The first course of action is to ask your library or information unit which services would be available to you as a member of the organisation. If none are available then it may be worth considering a personal or research group subscription, or following up free services from specific publishers.

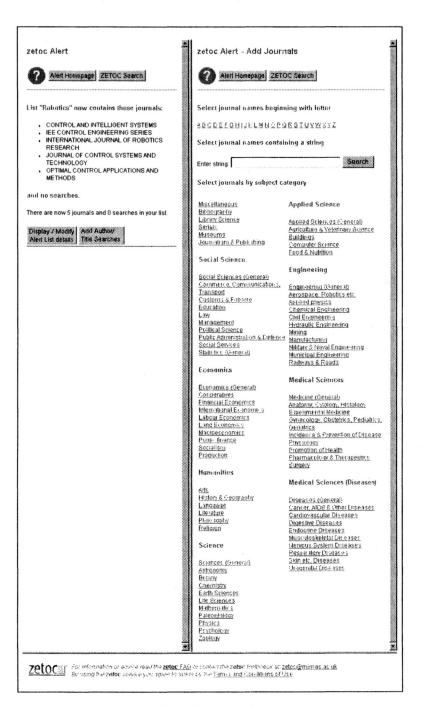

Figure 32: zetoc Alert

Current-awareness bulletins

Though these contents page services are very popular with researchers, there are other ways of keeping up to date with new papers published in journals. Some bibliographic databases will publish what are basically newsletters for the purpose of alerting researchers to new papers in specific, fairly narrow subject fields. These are actually very small subsets of the database – one of the major expenses of publication is in the compiling and indexing of the information. Once the database is in existence, the more end products which can be obtained the better.

These newsletters, known as current-awareness bulletins, are published under a variety of names. One of the best known is *CA Selects*, published by *Chemical Abstracts*. The *CA Selects* series covers more than 240 different topics, the bulletins being produced fortnightly in both printed and Web format. Bulletins such as *CA Selects* are really aimed at researchers, not libraries and information units. They are intended for immediate short-term use, not for searching back for information over several years.

Saved searches and autoalerts

Bibliographic databases can often also be used directly for keeping up to date, without needing to subscribe to a current-awareness bulletin. Normally a search strategy or history – the combination of keywords used during a search – are lost when the user logs off. However, it is often possible to save the search strategy on the service provider's computer system, the system allocating a unique number or code as an identifier. You can then log on to the database at regular intervals, and give instructions to match the search strategy against the updated database to find the latest articles on the topic. One of the benefits of this approach is that the search strategy can specify options not available via an ETOC service – for instance to retrieve papers containing specific keywords, whatever journals these may be published in.

The saved or stored search approach does mean having to remember to log in at regular intervals to run the keywords against the latest updates. With some services you can get round this problem by setting up an autoalert. This is a saved search which is automatically matched against records in the database at periodic intervals, with any newly added references emailed to you. The example shown in Figure 33 is a request screen for an OVID autoalert (SDI) for the *INSPEC* database on *EDINA* – the initials SDI stand for selective dissemination of information, another name for this type of current-awareness service.

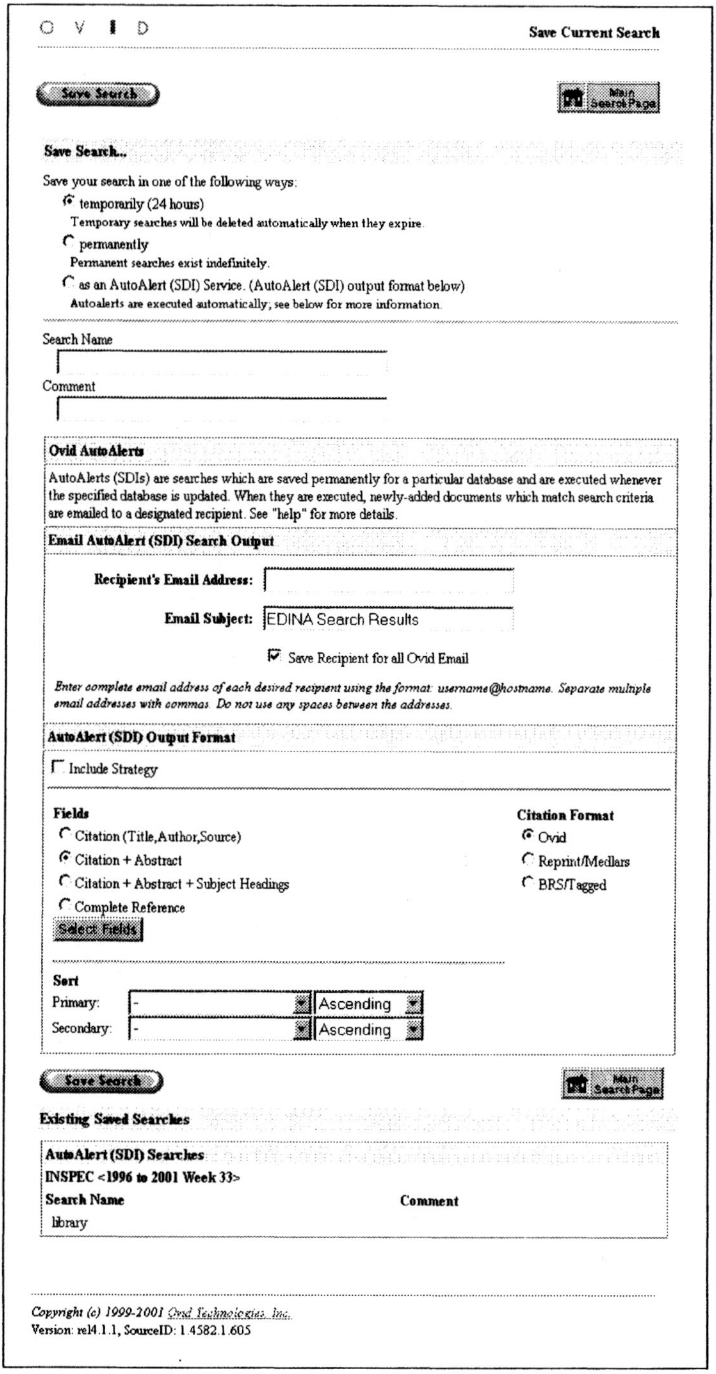

Figure 33: OVID save current search screen. (Used with the permission of the Institution of Electrical Engineers, EDINA and OVID Techologies Inc.)

Commercial versions of this type of service are also available – the big database producers such as *INSPEC* for instance also market their own SDI searches directly. The search strategies are generally compiled by the database producer's own staff, with subscribers completing a form to indicate their interests. There is obviously a direct cost involved in using commercial SDI services to keep up to date – for a new postgraduate or a lone research worker the price may be prohibitive, but reasonable where a team of people is working on a long-running project supported by adequate funding. Anyone using a commercial service does need to monitor the output regularly and modify the search strategy if appropriate – it is easy to allow this to become out of date as the subject interests gradually shift.

Research in progress

So far in this chapter we have concentrated on how you can keep up with the results of new research and development. However to get a complete picture of the activity within a speciality you really need some knowledge of what work is currently being carried out – projects which are in progress but about which little or nothing has yet been published. There are two good reasons why it is useful to have some idea of what is going on:

- it could prevent you duplicating someone else's work
- more positively, it might lead to some assistance, and/or co-operation with your project.

Obviously there are limits to how much you can find out – no one in a commercial organisation, such as a pharmaceutical company, for example, is going to reveal the direction of his or her research effort. Within the publicly supported sector – academic institutions and government-owned research establishments – there is more openness about current activities. The following information on discovering relevant projects consequently relates mainly to these areas.

Most people pick up a good percentage of their knowledge of current work through the 'grapevine' system, talking with friends and colleagues and going to seminars, conferences and the like. To supplement this approach, and for anyone without contacts within a subject field, there is a useful free Web site called *Nest* (*Network for the Exploitation of Science and Technology*) at *http://www.nest.ac.uk*, set up by the UK Research Councils. *Nest* includes projects funded by the following research councils:

- BBSRC – Biotechnology and Biological Sciences Research Council (*http://www.bbsrc.ac.uk*)

- CCLRC – Council for the Central Laboratory of the Research Councils (Rutherford Appleton and Daresbury Laboratories) (*http://www.clrc.ac.uk*)

- EPSRC – Engineering and Physical Sciences Research Council (*http://www.epsrc.ac.uk*)

- MRC – Medical Research Council (*http://www.mrc.ac.uk*)

- NERC – Natural Environment Research Council (*http://www.nerc.ac.uk*)

- PPARC – Particle Physics and Astronomy Research Council (*http://www.pparc.ac.uk*)

Some of the Research Councils, such as the EPSRC, also maintain their own databases of projects they are currently funding.

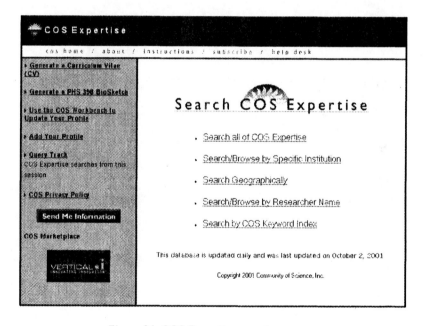

Figure 34: COS Expertise *search screen*

Figure 35: COS Expertise *results screen*

Patents

Improvements in or relating to diagnosis and treatment of bacterial infections, United Kingdom, Patent No. PCT/GB99/01650, 1999, Industry-owned. [Abstract] [USPTO Full-Text]

Publications

- Rafiq M, Worthington T, Tebbs SE, Treacy RB, Dias R, Lambert PA, Elliott TS. Serological detection of Gram-positive bacterial infection around prostheses. Journal of Bone and Joint Surgery, British Volume. 82(8): 1156-61, Nov 2000 [Abstract]

- Worthington T, Lambert PA, Elliott TS. Is hospital-acquired intravascular catheter-related sepsis associated with outbreak strains of coagulase-negative staphylococci?. Journal of Hospital Infection. 46(2): 130-4, Oct 2000 [Abstract]

- Littlewood JM, Koch C, Lambert PA, Holby N, Elborn JS, Conway SP, Dinwiddie R, Duncan-Skingle F. A ten year review of colomycin. Respiratory Medicine. 94(7): 632-40, Jul 2000 [Abstract]

- Elliott TS, Tebbs SE, Moss HA, Worthington T, Spare MK, Faroqui MH, Lambert PA. A novel serological test for the diagnosis of central venous catheter-associated sepsis. Journal of Infection. 40(3): 262-6, May 2000 [Abstract]

- Lang S, Livesley MA, Lambert PA, Elliott J, Elliott TS. The genomic diversity of coagulase-negative staphylococci associated with nosocomial infections. Journal of Hospital Infection. 43(3): 187-93, Nov 1999 [Abstract]

- Manzoor SE, Lambert PA, Griffiths PA, Gill MJ, Fraise AP. Reduced glutaraldehyde susceptibility in Mycobacterium chelonae associated with altered cell wall polysaccharides. Journal of Antimicrobial Chemotherapy. 43(6): 759-65, Jun 1999 [Abstract]

- Elliott TS, Lambert PA. Antibacterial resistance in the intensive care unit: mechanisms and management. British Medical Bulletin. 55(1): 259-76, 1999 [Abstract]

- Livesley MA, Tebbs SE, Moss HA, Faroqui MH, Lambert PA, Elliott TS. Use of pulsed field gel electrophoresis to determine the source of microbial contamination of central venous catheters. European Journal of Clinical Microbiology and Infectious Diseases. 17(2): 108-12, Feb 1998 [Abstract]

Profile Details

Last Updated: May 29, 2001

COS Expertise ID #497640
Reference this profile directly: http://myprofile.cos.com/P443921LAy

Individual Expertise profile of *Peter Anthony LAMBERT*. Copyright Peter Anthony LAMBERT.
© COS Expertise ™. Copyright Community of Science, Inc. 2001. All rights reserved.

Create a Document

Generate a curriculum vitae (CV).

Generate a PHS 398 Biographical Sketch for NIH.

Locate Funding

Listed below are the areas of interest for this individual. Use the check boxes to automatically search for related funding in the COS Funding Opportunities database

☐ Microbiology

Combine the terms selected above with ⦿ Or ⦿ And
Deadline within the next ⦿ 1 month ⦿ 2 months ⦿ 3 months ⦿ Deadline not important

[Locate Funding]

Figure 35: COS Expertise *results screen*

Another source of information is the *Community of Science (COS) Expertise (http://expertise.cos.com/)*. *COS Expertise* describes itself as a network of researchers, used for collaborative purposes by universities and research-driven organisations worldwide. As Figure 34 shows, information can be found by subject, institution or geographical location. Figure 35 shows part of a record from *COS Expertise*. Access is free to Association of Commonwealth University members, which includes UK universities. In the US the *Federal Research in Progress (FEDRIP)* database covers current government-funded research within the scientific and technological fields. *FEDRIP* does not provide a free service, but if you have a need your library or information unit may be able to arrange access to the database.

One note of warning about registers of current research. It is almost impossible to compile a complete list. Inevitably some people do not report their research and some projects may be excluded because of the classified nature of the research. You can never be certain that no one else is working in your field but you can be aware of who your major rivals might be.

Summary

- Check the Web pages of publishers in your subject field, asking to be emailed information on new books.
- Pick out the most important journals in your area, and check all new issues of them.
- Supplement this information by using electronic tables of contents services, or other current-awareness and SDI tools to keep you up to date with the latest articles in your subject field.
- Check *Community of Science* or other specialised databases of research in progress for other relevant projects.

Chapter 7

The future

So far we have concentrated on the current sources and methods you can use to find information. In this last chapter we would like to move on from current practices and consider the future. What are the prospects for the structure and communication of scientific, technical and medical information? To what extent will it be further affected by advances in information technology?

As we explained at the beginning of the book, information can be viewed from two different, though interrelated, aspects:

• how it is transmitted to the scientific, technical and medical community

• how the individual researcher searches out the information needed from the mass of material available.

Both are important – even if individuals do not generate new information, they will certainly use it and both aspects will undoubtedly be affected not just by greater use of IT but also market forces.

Journals

For well over 300 years now, scholarly journals have been the major means of communication of new scientific, technical and medical information to the world at large. Any discussion of the way information may be communicated in the future needs to consider their likely role. After a somewhat shaky start, the Web has enabled electronic journals – or to be more precise electronic versions of existing journals, also published in printed format – to take off. It seems certain that over the next decade most current titles will be published electronically, though whether print versions will also continue to be published is less clear.

One of the major issues relating to the development of scholarly journals is their cost. In 1999 for instance the average price of science and technology journals increased by 10.2%. [1] Nor was this an exceptional year – the same kind of increases were experienced throughout the 1990s. The problems for libraries and information units is that their budgets have tended to increase at the general rate of inflation, around 2 or 3% per annum. These year-on-year increases have inevitably stimulated interest in alternative approaches to communication, including those outlined overleaf.

• The development of free electronic archives. The success of the Los Alamos e-print server for the physics community has proved a spur to other subject fields. One instance of this is PubMed Central established by the US National Institutes of Health in 2000 (*http://www.pubmedcentral.nih.gov*). Journals are being asked to contribute articles on a voluntary basis to PubMed Central up to a year after publication, the intention being that publishers can make their profit by providing exclusive access in the first few months after publication when the demand is at its highest. Another initiative is BioMed Central, a commercial publishing company which has launched around fifty online biomedical journals (*http://www.biomedcentral.com*). Access to the articles is free, with BioMed Central intending to make their profit from activities such as commissioning reviews, alerting services and other ways of improving access to the "raw data". One question always raised in connection with electronic archives is that of refereeing. The articles available on both PubMed Central and BioMed Central will have been subject to peer review, but not all archives may develop this way.

• The development of new high-quality but low-priced journals, via the SPARC initiative (*http://www.arl.org/sparc*). SPARC – the Scholarly Publishing and Academic Resources Coalition – was set up in 1998 under the auspices of the US Association of Research Libraries, as a result of the frustration caused by the rising price of commercial journals. Over 180 libraries and other organisations are now members of SPARC including CURL – the Consortium of Research Libraries in the UK. One of the aims of SPARC is to promote competition by using libraries' purchasing power to encourage the setting up of new peer-reviewed titles at reasonable prices. SPARC has entered into partnership with a number of publishers, supporting the launch of a range of new journal titles, such as *Organic Letters,* as rivals to existing expensive titles.

Whether initiatives such as these will be successful on a large scale depends to a great extent on whether they can attract sufficient authors. One of the difficulties faced by any new journal is persuading researchers to submit papers to a publication without an established reputation. Another of SPARC's initiatives has been the setting up of BioOne, a non-profit collaboration of many small societies publishing bioscience journals. The BioOne database (*http://www.BioOne.org*) is actually an aggregate of existing prestigious research journals, so the issue of attracting authors should be less of a problem.

An alternative approach to the issue has been instituted by *HighWire Press*, a department of the Stanford University Libraries (*http://highwire.stanford.edu/*), mentioned in Chapter 5. *HighWire* can be described as an "Internet publishing service", acting as a host for the electronic versions of many scholarly journals. These include prestige titles such as the *Journal of Biological Chemistry*. Some journals such as the *British Medical Journal* are free from the point of publication. Other journals involved in *HighWire* have made back issues more than one year old free to access. One of the reasons for doing so is that the societies publishing the journals wanted to make a return to the scientific community responsible for producing the articles. Another reason is that most of the usage of articles on the Internet happens within a very short time after release. After six months only 7% of articles are read. As the income received after the first few months is so small, the publishers decided there was no reason to charge for use.

A further factor to be taken into consideration is the development of individual article delivery services. It has been recognised for quite a long time that only a small number of the articles published in some journals are likely to be of interest to researchers in an organisation. A library or information unit could be spending £3,000 or more on an annual subscription for which only 10 or so articles a year were needed by the unit's users. It is not an easy issue to confront, partly because of the difficulty of collecting statistics on usage of printed journals. There are now many more possibilities for researchers to obtain individual articles on demand straight to the desktop. The British Library's Document Supply Centre provides such a service and publishers too have started to sell individual articles directly via their Web sites, although at prices higher than the cost of traditional interlibrary loans. The development of the DOI or Digital Object Identifier – a unique way of identifying every article published – may help push these type of services forward.

E-books

While electronic versions of journals are now in widespread use, electronic or e-books have yet to become commonplace. Definitions of e-books vary but could basically be described as a text or monograph provided in electronic format. The reading devices range from hand-held computers and palmtops, through dedicated e-book readers, to standard PCs or laptops, with the appropriate software installed. E-books should provide benefits to users in terms of instant delivery to the desk top – being able to search the library catalogue over the Web has been a major step forward but it still involves a trek to the library to fetch and subsequently return an item. Although there are doubts about whether e-books can take off in the mass market, they do have the potential to be successful in academic and research environments.

Access to information

Looking at the second aspect of scientific, technical and medical information – how the individual worker finds relevant articles, patents, books, etc. from the mass of published material – one trend is towards greater integration of different resources. Although electronic access has made the task much easier, several different types of resources may be used during the course of a reasonably comprehensive search:

• the Web
• library catalogues and booksellers' sites
• bibliographic databases
• lists of journal titles.

The fact that there are several different access routes to information has obvious benefits, but there is also the risk that many – if not most – users get no further than the free Web sites found by the big search engines.

One of the developments likely to take place over the next few years is that these different types of resources will be integrated in a much more seamless way than at present – the "hybrid library" concept. One UK research project – Agora – has developed an interface enabling simultaneous searching across a whole range of resources, including

Figure 36 – Agora demonstrator project

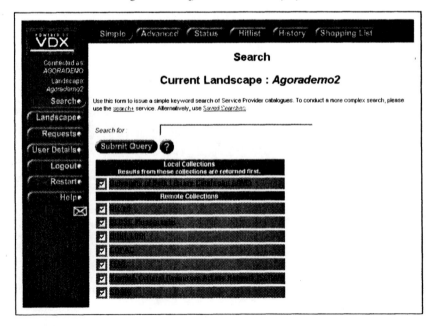

library catalogues, museum databases, archives, electronic journals, images, Web sites, search engines and online bookstores (Figure 36). Although Agora is a demonstrator project for the social sciences, there is every reason to expect similar approaches for scientific, technical and medical fields.

Another development in the pipeline is for libraries and information units to provide users with their own "personal information environments" or PIEs. In outward appearance these would be Web pages set up to give access to the library catalogue, subject gateways, bibliographic databases and other resources relevant to the particular subject interests of each user. Initially PIEs would be set up with links to a range of standard resources for a subject field, but with the user being able to customise this by adding or deleting resources over the course of time.

The future is also dependent on developments in information technology yet to be invented. When a previous edition of this book was published 10 years ago, the Web did not exist. In the space of a decade it has revolutionised the way we search for information. What is clear is that IT will continue to have an enormous impact on the generation, storage, and retrieval of information.

Reference

1. *Library & Information Statistics Tables 2000*. Loughborough, Leicestershire: Library & Information Statistics Unit (LISU), Loughborough University, 2000.

Index

abbreviations 13
abstracts 10–11
access, bibliographic databases 60–62
accuracy, evaluation of Web sites 27
Adobe Acrobat Reader software 89–91
aggregators 88–89
Agora research project 118–119
archives *see* electronic archives
arXiv 5
ATHENS usernames and passwords 62
authors' Web sites 1–2, 90
autoalerts 108–109

bibliographic databases 10–11
    choice of 54–59
    use of 44–86
bibliographic software, personal 95–96
Biblioscape 95, 100
BIDS 60
BioMed Central 116
BioOne 116
BLPC *see* British Library Public Catalogue
Bookends Plus 95, 100
books 9
    databases of 38
    new titles 103–104
    referencing 12
Boolean logic 17, 51–53, 62–63, 98
British Library Document Supply Centre 93–94, 117
British Library Public Catalogue 41
BUBL 20–22

CA Selects 108

catalogues *see* library catalogues

CD-ROM 61

Chemical Abstracts, Registry Numbers 50

Chemical Data Service 86

Chest 101

Citation (personal bibliographic software) 95, 100

Cite While You Write 96, 99

classification, Dewey Decimal 32

    use in searching bibliographic databases 48–50

classified directories, use of in searching the Web 20–23

Combined Higher Education Software Team *see* Chest

communication of information 1–11, 115–118

Community of Science see COS

comprehensiveness, evaluation of Web sites 28

conference proceedings 6

    referencing 12

controlled searching 63

COPAC 38–41

copyright legislation 94

COS 111–114

currency, evaluation of Web sites 28

current awareness bulletins 108

Current Contents 106

databanks 10–11

databases of published books 38

data centres 60–61

Dialog 85

digital dissertations 43

directories *see* classified directories

discussion lists

    communication of information 1–2

    referencing 14

document delivery *see* interlibrary loan

downloading 94

e-books 117

EDINA 61

    example search 70–78

    journals index display 59

    autoalert's (SDI) 108–109

    sample record 47

EEVL: the Internet Guide to Engineering, Mathematics and Computing
    24

electronic journals 5

    access 87–90

    library catalogues 37–38

electronic archives 5–6, 90–91, 116

electronic table of contents alerting services 105–107

email

    communication of information 1–2

    referencing 14

encyclopaedias 30

EndNote 95, 100

e-print archives *see* electronic archives

ESDU (Engineering Sciences Data Unit) 86

ETOCs *see* electronic table of contents alerting services

evaluation, Web sites 26–28

example searches 65–84

factual databases 10, 85–86

formatting records, personal bibliographic software 96

free text searching 63

future developments 115–119

Google 17–18

guides to the literature 32

handbooks 30

Harvard system, referencing 11

HighWire Press 91, 116

HTML format 90

Human Genome Project 10, 86
hybrid library 118

ILL *see* interlibrary loan
importing records, personal bibliographic software 97
indexing
    methods of 46
    personal bibliographic software 98
Index to Theses 41–3
information, communication of 1–11
ingenta Journals 89
Inside Alert 106
INSPEC
    example search 70–78
    journals index display 59
    OVID autoalert (SDI) 108–109
    sample record 47
interlibrary loan 91–94
International Standard Book Number 33
Internet Protocol *see* IP
IP addresses 62, 89
ISBN *see* International Standard Book Number

journals
    communication of information 3-5
    future developments 115–117
    library catalogues 36–8
    papers in press 5
    preliminary communications 3
    scanning new issues 105
    see also electronic journals *and* printed journals

keeping up to date 102–114
Kempe's Engineers Year–book 30–1
keywords
    choice of 53–54

library catalogues 34–35
    searching by 34–35
legislation, copyright 95
letter by letter, filing rules 34
library catalogues 32–8
    hyperlinks to 87
library Web pages 27
limits, use of in searching 64

M25 Access and Borrowing Scheme 91
mailing lists *see* discussion lists
mediated searching 85
Medical Subject Headings (MeSH) 48–49
MEDLINE see PubMed
MeSH see Medical Subject Headings (MeSH)
metasearch engines 20
MIMAS 61, 106
    example search 79–84
minus symbol, use of in searching the Web 17

NISS 60
    hyperlinks to library catalogues 87, 91
    links to bookshops and publishers 104
numeric system, referencing 12

OCLC FirstSearch browse index 54
offprints 90
output, personal bibliographic software 99
OVID autoalert (SDI) 108–109
    example search 70–78
    journals index display 59
    sample record 47

Papyrus 95, 100
passwords 61–2
patents 7–9

classification codes 48

referencing 12

searching for 85

PBM *see* personal bibliographic software

PDF *see* Portable Document Format

peer review 3, 6

people, communication of information 1

personal bibliographic software 96–102

personal information environments 120

personal literature collections, organisation 95–101

PIEs *see* personal information environments

planning a search 51–59

plus symbol, use of in searching the Web 17

Portable Document Format 89

Prentice-Hall electronic mailing list 103

pre-print servers 5–6

previously known work 15–6

printed journals, referencing 13

proceedings *see* conference proceedings

ProCite 95, 101

products, software 99–101

proximity searching 63–64

published books, databases of 38

PubMed

example search 66–69

links to full text 89

sample record 45

PubMed Central 6, 116

quotation marks, use of in searching the Web 17

RDN Virtual Training Suite 29

reciprocal borrowing schemes 91

record formats, personal bibliographic software 96–97

refereeing *see* peer review

referencing 11–14

Registry Numbers 50
reports 7
research in progress 110–114
Research Manager 95, 101
re-using groups of references 64
reviews 9–10

saved searches 65, 108–110
scanning journals 105
Scholarly Publishing and Academic Resources Coalition *see* SPARC
Science Citation Index
	example search 79–84
	links to full text 89
Scirus 19
SDI 108, 110
search engines 16–20
searching
	display of search history 64
	library catalogues 32–8
	order of display of records 65
	personal bibliographic software 97, 98
	planning 51–59
	refining a search 85–86
	retrieval software 62–65
	saved searches 110–12
	the Web 15–29
search software 62–65
selective dissemination of information *see* SDI
Smart Materials and Structures 4
SPARC 116
standards 9
	referencing 13
starting paper, *Science Citation Index* search 79
structure, bibliographic databases 44–47
subject gateways, use of in searching the Web 23–26

tables of contents, electronic 105–107
thesauri 46–48
theses 6, 41–43
tracing a paper forward in time 79
trade literature 9
truncation, use of in searching 64

Usenet newsgroups, communication of information 1–2
usernames 61–62

verbal information 1, 102–103
virtual libraries *see* subject gateways

Web
     communication of information 1–2
     evaluating sites 26–28
     referencing 13–14
     searching for information 15–29
Web of Science see Science Citation Index
word by word, filing rules 34

Z39.50 searching 97
zetoc Alert 106–107